# CONTROLS

Anatomy of an Accident

Fire was a forgotten danger until Berger crashed at Imola. The Austrian gave Alan Lis the inside story.

On the grid awaiting the start of the 1989 San Marino Grand Prix at Imola is Gerhard Berger in Ferrari 640 chassis 107. Berger is fully clothed in flame resistant boots, gloves and driving suit. He wears a fully enveloping crash helmet and has the visor up. A six-point harness holds him firmly in his seat. Mechanics hold a one-piece upper body section above his head as last-minute checks are made, affording him some shade from the bright sunshine.

The Ferrari is filled to the brim with AGIP fuel, which has been cooled to the permitted 10 degrees below ambient temperature. At this temperature the density of the liquid has increased sufficiently to enable an extra five litres to be squeezed into the car. The fuel is carried in a single flexible cell which is positioned in a tank behind the cockpit. Due to the length of the Ferrari V12 engine it has been necessary to expand the tank sideways beyond the width of the cockpit, and along the sides of it to avoid compromising the car's handling by having too long a wheelbase.

Insulating blankets are wrapped around the tyres in an effort to conserve the heat generated in the rubber during the warm-up laps of a few minutes earlier. The car has

been lifted off the ground and is balancing on two quick lift jacks. Now the upper bodywork is put in position where it is fastened by spring-loaded screws. An umbrella is held over Berger's head to continue shading him.

A horn blast ushers the supporting personnel for the grid. The tyre blankets are removed and the car is lowered onto the track surface.

Ferrari number 28 is fifth on the grid, in line astern behind a sister car driven by Nigel Mansell. The umbrella is folded and the V12 engine is churned into life by Berger's last remaining helpers. As they scurry off the soprano bark of its three and a half litres blends into the cacophony as another twenty-five cars and drivers similarly await the start of the parade lap.

The cars move off row by row. Berger holds station behind Riccardo Patrese in a Williams Renault. Going up the hill to the Piratella the Ferrari weaves from side to side as its driver re-heats the tyres.

Arriving back at the grid the front rows wait as stragglers get into position at the rear. The sound builds to a crescendo. The lights on the gantry flick red, a pause, then green. Pandemonium. The McLarens on the front row burst away with the pack snarling and snapping at their heels. Into the Tamburello. Berger motions to pass Mansell on the inside of the corner, but thinks better of it and falls into line behind his team mate. Boxed in behind Mansell, Berger is passed by Patrese. The Italian's Williams goes by as they exit Tamburello and race towards the Rettifilio.

Already the McLarens have distanced themselves from the rest of the field. At the first chicane – Acque Minerale – Mansell goes through cleanly. Patrese follows with Berger chasing hard and running front and rear tyres over the left hand kerb.

On the second lap Patrese attacks Mansell. Berger closes in as his team mate defends his position. Berger goes cleanly through the Acque Minerale, but on the final part of the Traguardo chicane which leads into the start area he clips another kerb. The back of the Ferrari slides out of line. Berger catches it.

On the third lap still hot on the heels of Williams Berger nudges the kerbs on the left and right at Acque Minerale. At the Traguardo he hits the kerb at the entry and runs wide, putting two wheels over the rumble strips at the exit.

Berger escaped lightly from the Ferrari fire at Imola. Only his hands were seriously injured.

Starting lap four Berger accelerates hard behind Patrese, glances to the right at his pitboard and passes under the Longines bridge. At the first corner, the McLarens long gone, spectators see Mansell, then Patrese, then Berger slam by.

The left front aerofoil on Berger's Ferrari shears at the point at which it is attached to the nose box. Deprived of downforce, the car instantly develops massive understeer as it enters the Tamburello for the fourth time, at over 150m.p.h. Berger brakes hard leaving long black tyre marks on the ashphalt. Thierry Boutsen following behind sees the Ferrari leave the track at barely diminished speed.

Anticipating a heavy impact, Berger takes his hands off the steering wheel and pulls his legs back as far as he is able. A spume of dust is flung up as the car crosses the grass run-off area. Turning slightly to the left, the Ferrari impacts the concrete wall with a force later estimated to have momentarily reached 50g.

Berger is knocked unconscious by the impact. Torn off its suspension mounts, the right front wheel is pushed back into the side pod. The destruction of the suspension dissipates some of the initial energy of impact but the rearward course of the wheel brings it into contact with the side located water radiator which is pushed along the side of the composite monocoque, peeling away the side mounted part of the fuel tank.

The inner rubber fuel cell tears by Berger's right shoulder and fuel sprays into the cockpit. Debris from the shattered right hand side of the Ferrari begins to fly into the air as the car scrapes along the wall beneath an advertising hoarding. The detached wheel bounces back onto the track.

Thirty metres further on from the point of initial impact the back of the Ferrari slides to the left, fuel leaking onto the grass and the car hits the wall a second time. It goes pirouetting through a further 540 degrees, shedding shrapnel and streaming fuel. At last it comes to rest, its rear end against the wall, facing the rest of the field streaming through the corner.

Beneath the fire-breathing emblem of AGIP, the Italian national fuel company, the Ferrari bursts into flames. The spilt fuel ignites the car's trail across the run-off area. Berger still is inside the wreck, still is unconscious and he is not connected to the car's life support system. Oxygen is burning away and fuel has penetrated his gloves. In

En route to disaster: Berger in the Ferrari 640 at Imola. Accelerating hard, the car lifts its nose.

places these are of only single layer construction. The leather palms shrink causing second degree burns to his palms.

Berger's four-layer driving suit is soaked in petrol but the outer layers protect him from the flames and he receives only chemical burns to the body from the refrigerated fuel. Within fifteen seconds an Alfa Romeo 164 fire tender arrives and a marshal wades into the fire with an extinguisher, directing it at the cockpit area. A second marshal attacks the seat of the fire and between them they manage to extinguish the flames in and around the car. Soon they are joined by further marshals who continue spraying the area with extinguishant to prevent re-ignition.

More help arrives.

The race is stopped.

Berger's condition is stabilised before he is removed from the remains of the car. He regains consciousness and is talking to his rescuers as he is loaded into an ambulance. He is taken to the circuit's medical centre where a broken rib and a minor fracture of the left shoulder blade are diagnosed. Removed to the Maggiore hospital in Bologna, Berger remains only a few hours before discharging himself. He is flown back to Austria for further specialist treatment.

He misses the Monaco Grand Prix, attending only as a spectator.

There is speculation as to his replacement in the Ferrari team.

Berger returns for the next race in Mexico City. His hands bandaged, he qualifies sixth fastest...

I

ACKNOWLEDGEMENTS

The authors are very grateful to the numerous individuals who took time and trouble to assist in the preparation of this book.

Special thanks to:

John Barnard
Gerhard Berger
Fiona Butterfield
Dennis Carlson
Darrell Cousins
Professor E. S. 'Sid' Watkins
Keith Greene
Tony James
David Kennedy
Ray Mallock
Gordon Murray
Steve Nichols
Ian Phillips
Eric Silbermann
Alan Staniforth
Nigel Stroud
Martin Whitaker

COMPETITION CAR

CONTROLS

CONTROLS & INSTRUMENTATION
DRIVER SAFETY & SUPPORT SYSTEMS
CLOTHING·COMMUNICATION·COOLING

IAN BAMSEY & ALAN LIS

Foulis

A **FOULIS** Motoring Book
First Published 1990
© RACECAR ENGINEERING 1990

Published by:
Haynes Publishing Group, Sparkford, Near Yeovil,
Somerset BA22 7JJ, England.

Haynes Publications Inc.
861 Lawrence Drive, Newbury Park, California, 91320,
USA.

Produced for G. T. Foulis & Co. Ltd. by
RACECAR ENGINEERING
Telephone and Fax: Yeovil (0935) 31295

Editorial Director: Ian Bamsey
Research Assistant: Alan Lis

British Library Cataloguing in Publication Data

Bamsey, Ian
Race car technology
1. Racing cars. Control and safety systems.
I. Title
629.2'43

ISBN 0-946132-61-5

Library of Congress Catalog Card number 89-84708

Printed in England by:
Wincanton Litho, Wincanton, Somerset
Typesetting & Artwork by:
Photosetting, Yeovil, Somerset

CONTENTS

The Professional Approach

Are controls, safety and support systems afterthoughts in Formula One terms? Ian Bamsey sought Gordon Murray's view.

Gordon Murray has been involved in the design and development of Grand Prix cars for the best part of two decades, primarily with Brabham though lately as Technical Director of McLaren International. Throughout he has been renowned as an innovator, and as an engineer dedicated to safety. "Formula One is at the sharp end of technology," he reflects, "in the design office you are at war with others in a similar position and unless something is restricted by regulations you tend to push it. But you have a moral obligation to consider safety." Murray points out that the prevailing technical regulations do not, cannot, ensure car safety as designers relentlessly push boundaries forward. Regulations have to chase the development of technology: in any pioneering situation safety has to be the responsibility of the individual pathfinder, who must set his own limits. Murray cites as example the development of the advanced composite monocoque. At the outset the use of advanced composites was unrestricted by regulations, and there was no experience of how they would perform in an accident. Formula One designers had to use personal judgement as to whether a given application would provide an acceptable margin of safety.

'We had a lot of practical experience of aluminium tubs crashing,' Murray explains, 'and we used that to make our cars safer. With the introduction of carbon fibre we lacked such experience. At Brabham we were initially leading in the exploitation of carbon fibre by two years yet we were one of the last to field a fully-advanced composite tub. It was purely caution."

Murray discovered carbon fibre in 1977 and in '78 he incorporated carbon fibre panels in the monocoque of his BT48. In 1979 he increased the percentage of carbon fibre for the BT49 tub from around 25% to around 50%. However, he was unwilling to drop an aluminium base until there was more knowledge of the new material. As a result in 1980 McLaren and Lotus had the glory of fielding the first uncompromised advanced composite monocoques. Meanwhile Murray talked Brabham team-owner Bernie Ecclestone into crash testing a complete BT49 model, using the extensive test facilities of new partner BMW.

'The crash test proved that carbon fibre worked well in some areas, badly in others,' Murray reports: 'we were able to adjust our thinking in the light of that.'

Always very conscious of the importance of driver safety, Murray is surprisingly critical of the recent pedals behind the front axle line dictate. This, he reasons, adds nothing to safety, so he sees it as an unwarranted restriction upon the designer. Murray's view is that the position of the driver's feet is immaterial in terms of safety – what is important is the structural integrity of the monocoque and of the nosebox. The nosebox has to conform to tight criteria and has to be crash tested. If the driver's feet are moved forward, the nosebox goes forward. Meanwhile, says Murray, the position of his feet in relation to the front wheels is barely relevant in terms of protection.

What is important is the concept of a survival cell, a concept Murray is very much in favour of. Consequently, he is appalled by moves to drop the requirement for longitudinal box sections in the chassis. Flanking the cockpit, such box sections were an integral feature of the first proper monocoque Grand Prix car, Colin Chapman's Lotus 25. Essentially, the pioneering Lotus tub consisted of two longitudinal torsion boxes held firmly in relation to one another via bulkheads, with further rigidity added by a stressed engine. Clearly, the original monocoque was not a single tube structure with a cockpit opening but that is just what many advanced composite tubs have become.

Whereas the original Lotus carried its fuel in its box section members, these days fuel is carried in a central tank. Further, advanced composite materials allow construction of a single tube with extremely high rigidity in spite of the necessity for a central cockpit opening. Such a structure in aluminium would have badly lacked torsional rigidity but these days with high stiffness fibre and plastic composites longitudinal box sections are virtually redundant. Worse, they are an obstacle when it comes to the production of a monocoque of minimal cross-sectional area.

In recent years a number of designers have conveniently forgotten to incorporate longitudinal box sections and rather than remind them, FISA has overlooked enforcing its survival cell criteria to the letter. The negligent body has now proposed to drop the requirement for box members in favour of monocoque rather than merely nosebox crash testing.

Murray points out that crashing head on, as in the proposed test, and crashing at any sort of angle, are very different matters. Hitting head on is a straight compression impact whereas any form of angled impact brings a bending load. That tests the beam stiffness of the monocoque. Box sections might not add significantly to the torsional rigidity of an advanced composite tub but they do provide massive beam stiffness. Thus, they can be invaluable in terms of helping stop the front of a car splitting asunder.

A monocoque can be designed to pass a frontal compression test without enjoying significant beam stiffness. 'Experience has proved you don't need much of an accident to break a monocoque that does not have longitudinal box sections,' Murray insists: 'the chances of crashing head on are pretty much nil. Formula One accidents tend to be at some sort of angle. Box sections provide massive beam stiffness and that means the front of the car does not fall off. To drop the requirement for box sections is a huge step backwards.'

When it comes to the question of driver comfort, Murray considers this another aspect of design that is of 'paramount importance. In Formula One driving is very violent. The driver has to work automatically and as quickly and as consistently as possible. If there is anything in the controls that he is not 100% happy with he will either go slowly or off the road.'

Murray explains that he always takes a lot of trouble with wooden mock-ups at the design stage, to give the driver an idea of what he will experience. He notes that, for example, the driver must be able to attack the steering wheel without his elbow hitting anything. If it should rub he will be in line for a massive bruise and consequently he will soon be instinctively holding his elbow in. That means he will not be getting the same feel through the steering. 'There must be the right amount of clearance to work the controls as quickly as required.'

The pedals must be positioned where the feet naturally fall, the clutch must not be awkward, the gear change must not be notchy. These are factors that slow a driver down in any racing situation, Murray opinions. 'Even in a road car an awkward clutch detracts from concentration,' he notes.

Murray found the pioneering 1989 Ferrari clutchless transmission: 'wonderful in theory but suffering serious drawbacks in practice. The system was very heavy and very complex. Berger's endless retirements were largely down to gearbox peripherals.'

Steering, in general terms, 'must be precise and direct. The system must be rigid enough so that the information it imparts to the driver remains accurate with downforce loadings. Formula One downforce can be around three tons at high speed. The steering must be rigid enough not to deflect under such a load.'

Murray sees no call for power assisted steering, as tried by Ligier in 1988. 'Steering weight is not a problem. All contemporary cars are the same weight and have the same weight distribution, the same tyres and the same level of downforce. All teams should be able to provide acceptable steering!'

Intriguingly, though, Murray reveals: 'there can be a problem of high downforce causing unacceptably high steering load. There is a simple trick to unload the steering but some designers have not yet twigged it.'

Pressed further, Murray admits that rack mounting is part of the answer. With his BT52 the rack was incorporated in a cast module carrying the front suspension. 'That was about as rigid as you can get. And that car had good steering...'

Brakes? 'That is the most difficult area of controls in

The control centre of a modern Formula One car. This is the 1990 Lotus-Lamborghini.

which to achieve consistency. The throttle tends to stay the same while there is very little clutch wear – and with a carbon-carbon clutch there is virtually no change from the start to the finish of a race. But with brakes there are variables in terms of pad wear, fluid viscosity and air penetration.'

As the pads wear there is more chance of knock-off and more pedal movement. Murray feels that the main consideration is for a pedal that is reasonably consistent without needing massive pressure. Unfortunately, it is a fact of life that a harder pedal tends to be more consistent at the expense of feel.

Murray notes that the brake pedal must stop in the right position to allow the driver to heel and toe. Another key consideration that Murray points to is the weight of the throttle. 'The driver might have his throttle pressed right to the floor for 20 or 30 seconds. That is a lot of muscular effort.' Murray explains that, applying a lot of pressure, a driver can get a form of temporary local paralysis without being aware of it. His foot then may well tell him he is at full throttle on the straight when in fact he is easing off slightly.

At the other extreme is the danger of a very light throttle, too easily disturbed over bumps. Take the Osterreichring. Long, sweeping corners demand a steady state throttle. If the throttle is too light its setting can be disturbed over bumps, and all too easily. The power variation can in turn affect the stability of the chassis. 'Throttle weight is much more important than people think,' Murray concludes.

Another important factor is instrument siting. 'You don't want too much eyeball travel,' Murray insists: 'At high speed there isn't time to refocus between the instruments and the track 100 yards ahead.' Murray takes the view that the driver doesn't have time to read numbers. 'That was why we had the upright needle system in the old days. These days we have LED displays which change colour.'

When it comes to mirrors, Murray feels it is important for a driver to have a proper three-quarter rear vision, primarily to be aware of any challenger's line of attack.

In Formula One cockpit cooling tends not to be a problem in Europe but can become a challenge elsewhere. It is generally a case of drilling holes. 'The cockpit is a natural low pressure area. If you drill a hole to bleed air in

In the late Eighties Murray was Technical Director of the super-successful McLaren International team. Here team drivers Senna and Prost lead the 1989 Monaco Grand Prix.

from an area of high pressure it will find its own way out through the top opening. The through flow is important.'

In general terms, Murray is in favour of the provision of a properly-designed drinks bottle system, since a dehydrated driver cannot be expected to function well. He notes that a crude system with the driver sucking from a bottle mounted on the dash would be upset by the heavy 'g' forces and that, for example, an acceleration of one 'g' would see a head of fluid arriving uninvited at the driver's mouth. Thus, a system incorporating a pump and one-way valves is essential. 'Provision of a drinks bottle is not as easy as it seems.'

A life support system Murray sees as 'good in theory, and certainly good in days gone by. But the triggering system is critical, and unless there is a reliable automatic trigger, these days it is perhaps a waste of time. The circuits are shorter and there are more marshals' posts. Most drivers don't like the tube flapping about. Over the years there have been experiments with accelerometer triggering but that has proved haphazard. The 'g' forces the car generates in normal running are very high. The problem is one of practicality. An unconscious driver cannot operate a life support system. And a marshal's time is likely to be better employed putting the fire out.'

Murray points to the same triggering problem with on-board fire extinguishers. Further, he recalls having seen two instances of exploding fire extinguishers in his time: 'Andretti blew the front off his car, Watson blew the wing assembly off.' In both cases overheating was to blame. The admittedly remote danger of explosion is something to bear in mind when siting an extinguisher, he reflects . . .

Seat belts, 'should be as good as possible. During our crash test of the BT49 the dummy driver was strapped in by a six-point racing harness. The car impacted a concrete block at 50k.p.h. and the driver moved forward enough for his head to touch the steering wheel. That was a combination of belt stretch and neck deflection.'

Moving on to the subject of radio communication, this is favoured by Murray. 'I introduced it at McLaren – Barnard didn't use it. The main benefit is being able to communicate on race strategy. In general, though, we try to use it as little as possible.'

Setting Safety Standards

Professor Sid Watkins is FISA's top medical man. Alan Lis asked him for his views on racing safety.

Professor E. S. 'Sid' Watkins, son of a Liverpool motor trader, qualified as a doctor in 1952. After National Service he began attending race meetings at various British circuits, initially as an official doctor before becoming a Medical Officer. In 1962 he moved to a hospital at Syracuse in Upper New York State and became Medical Officer at Watkins Glen and various other circuits in the United States.

After eight years Stateside, Watkins returned to England and in 1970 he was invited by Dean Delamont to join the RAC medical commission, becoming the club's Neurosurgeon. During this period his work at British race meetings brought him into contact with the International Grand Prix Medical Unit. This was a mobile hospital introduced by Louis Stanley after regrettable inadequacies in medical standards had been highlighted by a number of accidents in the mid-Sixties, including Jackie Stewart's crash in a BRM at Spa in 1966. Watkins found it a tremendous facility.

As Professor Watkins explained in an interview in *Autosport* in 1984; 'The idea of making a resuscitation facility of that order available was a very good concept indeed. The problem was, moving it from country to country caused emotional reactions at certain circuits... It produced a tremendous amount of interest and controversy but it did highlight the problem of medical facilities at the races.'

The 'Stanley Wagon', as the Unit became known, led to the realisation that circuit medical facilities could be much improved. Meanwhile, an increasingly professional image was being projected for the sport by the emergent Formula One Constructors' Association. In 1978 the F.O.C.A. President, Bernard Ecclestone, appointed Watkins surgical advisor to F.O.C.A. and asked him to attend all races to look after the medical welfare of the drivers.

In some countries Watkins' appointment proved to be an unpopular move, in particular provoking indignation from certain Chief Medical Officers, who saw it as calling their facilities into question. In October 1981, after a sometimes difficult three years, FISA recognised the good work done and appointed Professor Watkins as the President of its newly-formed Medical Commission. The FISA appointment, initially for three years, recently reached the eighth-year mark.

Professor Watkins presides over a commission which sets the medical standards in all motorsport. Watkins also has a personal responsibility as a FISA medical delegate to inspect facilities and ensure the maintenance of standards at Grands Prix meetings. A colleague, Dr. Isserman, carries out similar inspections for events outside of the Formula One sphere, such as Group C and Formula 3000.

Certain basic medical facilities have to be provided and other requirements met before a FISA-sanctioned event can take place. Each circuit staging a meeting must have a permanent medical centre, equivalent to a critical care unit such as that found in a large university or teaching hospital. The centre has to be staffed with anaesthetists and surgeons capable of providing first-class medical opinion and management when necessary.

The organisers of an international meeting must also provide fast medical intervention in response to an accident, with teams equipped to enable resuscitation and assessment of injury in the car, to allow safe removal without adding injury. This may involve cutting open a car. It is further required that facilities should be on hand to effect rapid evacuation by helicopter or ambulance to a designated hospital, the facilities of which will also have been inspected before the event. Inspections and agree-

Professor Sid Watkins attends Grand Prix races as FISA's medical supervisor. He has seen circuit facilities improve dramatically.

ments on these provisions are made anually, ensuring that standards are maintained. The responsibility for arranging these facilities and their cost is borne by the National Sporting Club of the country in which the event is held.

Prior to the inception of the Medical Commission, medical facilities at some events were of a very low standard. In some instances there was nothing more than a Red Cross tent; more suited to a garden fete than an international sporting event. Permanent buildings were considered the first basic and important step on the road to the current position. Interviewed at the 1989 Italian Grand Prix meeting, Professor Watkins expressed himself now to be opposed to an 'elitist' travelling unit such as the International Grand Prix Medical Unit. 'Rather than using a travelling unit, it was felt that it would be better to develop permanent facilities at each circuit. The mobile unit provided a service for Formula One but did not establish a tradition. There was no legacy left behind when the circus moved on. Today the facilities provided for a Grand Prix remain for the use of the rest of the sport.'

Medical legislation is made by FISA in conjunction with its Safety Commission. Professor Watkins explained; "as you can appreciate, the monitoring of medical standards, of injuries and accidents, is very important with regard to car and circuit safety. If the recommendations made by the Medical Commission are endorsed by the FISA Executive the subsequent regulation will become established as law.'

Watkins points out that such a procedure allows action to be taken quickly. At the 1989 Phoenix Grand Prix meeting a potential hazard with freon gas-operated personal cooling systems came to light and legislation outlawing such systems was approved and imposed before the next Grand Prix.

A system exists to prevent drivers racing if unfit, Watkins explains. After an injurious accident a driver's international medical card is withdrawn by the Chief Medical Officer of the event. In order to race again at that or any subsequent meeting the driver must be reintegrated. If admitted to hospital a driver must undergo examination by an appropriate consultant. In such a case his medical card would be returned to his National

Sporting Club who would then be responsible for his re-integration.

In the event of minor injuries the Chief Medical Officer at an event can re-integrate a driver. For example, on Gerhard Berger's return to racing after his Imola accident, his re-integration procedure was carried out at the circuit in Mexico City after examination at the medical centre. As a further safeguard, the Clerk of the Course and Stewards at an event can request the examination of a driver and obtain a written statement as to the individual's fitness to race. There is thereby strict control of whether a driver is permitted to race or not. After a high-speed accident the regulatory system ensures that a driver is examined even if he appears to have escaped lightly.

A to Z

Boots

As Jackie Stewart says, 'your feet should not be forgotten because you're pressing pedals all the time. In a Grand Prix car the right foot is never off the accelerator or the brake pedal.' Stewart, in fact, reports (in his book *Principles of Competition Driving*) that he had a lot of trouble with a nerve in the ball of his right foot that was very close to the surface and was consequently easily inflamed by pressure, causing great pain. Eventually he had the nerve cut and blocked off but the pain didn't disappear entirely and it was one of the reasons why he did little long-distance racing. It led him to wear Hush Puppies with thick soles and he says that those soles didn't appear to lose him any sensitivity.

Today such footwear would be rejected by Formula One scrutineers. FISA regulations require that footwear should cover the entire foot and ankle. Like all peripherals, boots must have been tested to the ISO 6940 test standard for flammability to comply with the FIA Safety Commission regulations. All laces and fastenings are required to be fire resistant and the sole has to be fire and hydrocarbon (i.e. petrol) resistant.

Most drivers wear Nomex-lined leather boots with thin asbestos/rubber soles. Some manufacturers favour thin leather soles. Thin soles were once thought to give a better feel on the pedals and today are favoured since they occupy less space in a cramped footwell. However, they are prone to wearing out very quickly should the driver neglect to change his footwear before making his round of visits in the paddock, or should mechanical frailty necessitate too many long walks back from far-flung reaches of the circuit.

Fire resistant socks are a must (as discussed in the Race Suit and Underwear sections) and it is sensible to wear fire resistant boots as well. In the event of a fire the feet are likely to be down in among it for longer than the rest of the body. Leather alone shrinks and burns. And the foot is highly susceptible to burn injuries.

Aside from fire resistance, heat resistance can be a factor to consider, particularly if the car is front-engined. Even a mid-engined car with a front radiator can be a

Feet don't fail me now . . . your boots are never off the pedals while driving.

nightmare, as Porsche discovered at Le Mans in 1977 when it reclined its drivers a little more than usual, pushing the pedals forward. The heat roasted the drivers' feet and asbestos boots were among the remedies tried!

Foot comfort should have a high priority: a driver should try all available fire-resistant boots before making a choice. An inner sole can help make a boot more comfortable and can act as a barrier to heat. Whatever boots or shoes are worn, it is essential to check that there are no projections that can snag on the pedals. Indeed, there should be no part of the boot, including any accessory, that can get caught on anything.

As a general rule, where specialist gear is not employed, footwear should be well broken-in before it is worn in the car. Rally drivers should slip on rubber overshoes when leaving the car in messy conditions. That avoids the danger of getting back in with damp, greasy footwear that is liable to slip off the pedals.

Feeling the strain: endurance racing is taxing and comfortable footwear is a must.

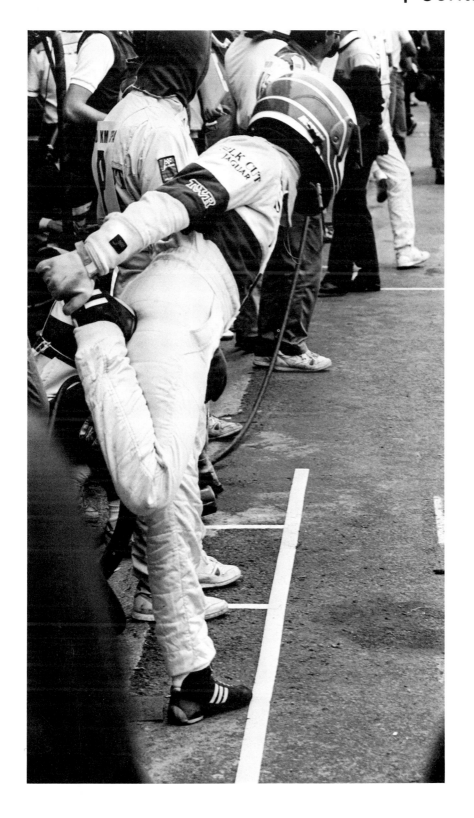

Brakes

The competition car industry has developed off the shelf disc brake systems to suit all applications. Drum brakes are a thing of the past: anyone contemplating any form of serious competition should fit a purpose designed competition system for reliability and effectiveness. Conventional competition car disc brake systems are well proven high quality products which are highly dependable. Lack of due care and maintenance is the only condition under which failure becomes a serious threat. However, even the most meticulous person can make a slip – the classic example is putting a pad in the wrong way around so that the metal back plate contacts the disc. Brake failure is arguably the greatest threat of all to a driver's safety and the onus is on a driver to ensure that his brakes have been properly looked after.

Invariably competition systems are dual circuit, with side by side master cylinders. In other words, the pedal operates separate master cylinders each with its own piping system for the front and rear brakes. Combined with a self-locking balance bar this ensures that failure of one system does not spell total brake failure. Nevertheless, retaining brakes at one end is no guarantee that the car will stay on the track...

Brake plumbing is a potential source of danger since line failure means instant brake failure. The plumbing should use the highest grade steel tubing and hoses of braided stainless wire with Teflon for added protection, together with aircraft nuts and fittings. All brake lines need to be protected from heat and vibration and must be routed to avoid damage from bending, chafing or crimping. Professionally built racing cars invariably have safe brake plumbing but the amateur builder must ensure that his brake lines are up to standard and are carefully routed. He must also ensure that the hard worked brake pedal is man enough for the job and that the pedal and master cylinders are securely mounted on a rigid bulkhead.

The driver must look after his brakes out on the track and this means carefully bedding in new pads and new discs as recommended by the supplier. Indeed, a heavy

Heavy duty braking system: two twin pot calipers grip a well ventilated cast iron disc.

application of pads that haven't been bedded properly can supply an exciting trip into the scenery. Brake fade caused by lack of proper pad bedding is known as 'green fade', and this should not be confused with fade caused by overheated pads or boiling fluid. Given conventional cast iron brakes and copper-asbestos pads, as a rule new pads and new discs should not be bedded in together. The driver should not use any set of pads, new or old, too hard before they have reached working temperature and the compound has stabilised. And he should make a cooling off lap whenever possible prior to parking in the pits so as to avoid the danger of heat soak overheating the pads or boiling the fluid. Further, since the exposed part of the disc will cool faster, parking with hot brakes can lead to disc cracking.

Fade caused by over-heated pads or boiled fluid will occur on the track only if cooling is inadequate, and there is a danger of a spectacular disc explosion. Following manufacturer guidelines should avoid such potential disasters. To repeat: provided a competition brake system is properly installed and cared for reliability is not a worry. However, for good brake performance it is necessary to ensure the correct front to rear proportioning for the conditions as well as the appropriate amount of cooling for the given circuit. Further, these days there exists the options of carbon-metallic pads on cast iron discs or carbon-carbon pad and discs sets to improve braking potential. Since brakes play such a vital role in driver safety a Special Investigation in another section of the book looks at the entire subject in depth.

Chassis

The modern Grand Prix car/Sports-Prototype/Indy Car is closer to a low-flying aircraft than a motor car in the conventional sense. Aerodynamic considerations dominate chassis design and downforce is so great that, for example, a typical late Eighties Sports-Prototype could run upside down on the ceiling at speeds in excess of 130m.p.h.!

That level of downforce takes a car out of the realms of conventional vehicle dynamics; for example, suspension theory as applied to road cars is barely relevant. The high downforce race car has hardly any ground clearance and no appreciable suspension movement (certainly less than two inches), since minimal clearance improves the effectiveness of its crucial underwing, while pitch and roll impairs underwing operation. A low-running, stiffly sprung, high downforce car can be thrown into a corner with an aplomb that would send a conventional vehicle rolling into the bushes. It doesn't tip over since it is being squashed into the ground by its own massive download. However, a kerb that would bounce a road car can flip a virtually suspension-less racing car that is all-but rubbing the ground.

Philippe Streiff found out all about that at Rio early in 1989 when his AGS hit a kerb. The car spun across the bevelled kerb and the kerbing acted like a ramp, launching it into the air. Strieff owes his life to the structural integrity of his car.

It appears that Gerhard Berger's horrifying high-speed shunt at Imola a few months later during the San Marino Grand Prix was triggered by his Ferrari's left front wing striking a kerb on a couple of occasions. Hitting a kerb with a wing endplate actually lifted the front wheels off the ground! The over-stressed wing support subsequently collapsed under high load – i.e., at high speed – and Berger was a passenger as his car failed to negotiate the 150m.p.h. Tamburello curve. The V12 Ferrari ploughed straight on and hit the concrete wall on the outside of the run-off area.

Its left front wing broken, Berger's car had fallen from the metaphorical ceiling... Having impacted at high

Special production: the Richard Lloyd Racing aluminium honeycomb chassis for the Porsche 962.

speed, the Ferrari slewed around and then slithered along the wall for about 200 yards before coming to rest. Moments later it exploded in flames. Fire was a hazard that Formula One had felt itself somewhat immune to following the development of immensely strong advanced composite material chassis.

Berger's carbon-fibre-skinned composite chassis had done a first-class job of protecting its occupant from impact injury. The following day Berger told Stan Piecha, 'All I could do was take my hands off the steering wheel and fold them across my chest. If you keep them on the wheel your arms and hands are more likely to be broken on impact. The monocoque of the car stood up tremendously. Often, when you have a high-speed crash your legs turn blue with bruises. My legs are fine. They don't even ache.'

The Ferrari's so-called 'survival cell' had remained intact, as it had been designed to do. While Berger's monocoque did not fail him as he thumped the wall – and he suffered no more than a damaged shoulder blade and rib – it appears that a forward projection of the fuel tankage alongside the cockpit (on the righthand side) was ruptured by the adjacent side radiator which in turn was pushed back by the collapsing right front corner. Hence the fire.

Berger was doused in chilled fuel – the fuel had been refrigerated so as to squeeze more into the available tankage – and as a consequence he suffered chemical burns. The fire, in which the car was engulfed pending the swift arrival of the fire services, caused only second degree burns to one hand. The fire was extinguished within 30 seconds and Berger thankfully did not inhale any fumes. Clearly, though, he owed his life to the prompt action by the emergency services, a point he was quick to gratefully emphasise.

Why did the tank apparently become ruptured by the radiator? In any high speed impact the corners of a car should progressively collapse to help dissipate energy. The energy of a crashing car has to be dissipated in some way or another and for this reason long shunts are potentially less harmful than short shunts. Since the late Seventies Formula One cars have typically carried a single central fuel tank, this incorporated in the back of the monocoque tub behind the survival cell. A lack of crash fires proved this to be the ideal location for the fuel load.

Aftermath: Brundle's Tyrrell after its dramatic Monaco '84 roll, pictured overleaf. This is a survival cell...

However, the re-emergence of side tanks, as featured on the '89 Ferrari 640 followed a new ruling for 1989 which demanded that the driver's feet be kept behind the front wheel axis.

Faced with this new dictate and a long V12 engine, Ferrari found it could not keep all its fuel behind the cockpit and retain an acceptable wheelbase length. Hence the side tanks, the danger of which was so vividly illustrated at Imola. At the time of writing, FISA was considering a mandatory return to central tankage. This would handicap a V12 runner. Ferrari designer John Barnard is very safety-conscious. He told *RaceCar Engineering* 'With the current cars now so narrow in the cockpit all safety considerations are very important. Any obstruc-

Over she goes: Brundle crashes out during qualifying for the '84 Monaco Grand Prix at Tabac.

tions inside the car can harm the driver in an accident as the legs fly around under the high g forces. I was pleased with the performance of the cockpit in this respect in the Imola accident as there was no injury to the driver's legs. The F640 was designed with a very clean interior, a lot of importance was placed on having no protruding bulkheads.'

As with an air crash, all pieces of the wrecked Ferrari were analysed by inspectors, some in fact from the aircraft industry. There were some interesting discoveries. As Barnard explained: "After the accident the cockpit area was found to be basically intact although the area around the fuel tank was found to be heavily damaged.

'The front of the chassis looked normal but closer inspection revealed that it was covered with stress fractures indicating that the energy from the accident had been diffused over the whole monocoque.'

Further energy from the accident would have been dissipated by the shedding of the front wheel, which tore off at the suspension pick-up points. The suspension is specifically designed to do this without damage to the pick-up, which makes the car relatively easy to repair as long as other damage is minor.

The inspection carried out after the accident also estimated the g loads exerted on various components, the monocoque itself was thought to have encountered 50 g on impact.

Speaking at the Spanish Grand Prix towards the end of the 1989 season Barnard explained that the investigation was basically complete, however, all parts had been retained for future reference if this should be necessary.

Another consequence of the '89 Formula One regulations was the cramped cockpit. In the Seventies and early Eighties, Grand Prix cars exploited ground effect tunnels and used front and rear wings as 'trim tabs' since underbody downforce is won at the lower drag penalty. Then, for 1983, came the flat bottom ruling, whereby the underbody had to form a flat surface within the wheelbase. It was still possible to win a measure of ground effect by accelerating air across the flat bottom area into a diffuser section positioned behind the rear wheel axis, but the rear wing assumed a renewed importance.

In view of that, Gordon Murray designed the 'lay down' Brabham BT55 which set its in-line four cylinder BMW engine on its side and reclined its driver to a degree unheard of since the low power Grand Prix cars of the early Sixties. For complex reasons the Brabham BT55 could not demonstrate its aerodynamic potential on the track but the advantage of an improved airflow to the rear wing was obvious to Murray in the wind tunnel. He subsequently joined McLaren and oversaw a low-line version of the Honda-McLaren turbocar, the MP4/4 of 1988.

The Honda V6 was fitted with a small, 5½-inch clutch which allowed a lower sump and with shorter inlet trumpets, thanks to higher r.p.m. running. The entire engine and fuel tank package was designed to be as low as possible, aided by a mandatory 150 litre tank maximum. The driver was reclined in the manner of the BT55. Although the central fuselage of the car kept to the same height as that of the Brabham, with a more conventional (V6) engine in the back the car did not look as radical. Appearances can be deceptive: the rear wing was again running in cleaner air, the wind tunnel figures were just as good as those for the original BT55 design and the level of downforce had taken a significant step forward. Murray commented to Allan Staniforth: 'it's a very simple car, very low with a good aerodynamic package. It has a lot of good flow to the rear wing and low frontal area. Chapman laid the driver right back – it's not a new idea, and drivers will never sit up again.'

At the same time March designer Adrian Newey devised the super-slim fuselage to help the airflow down the flanks of the car. At some races the Marches lost their clutches since the drivers unavoidably rode them – there was nowhere to rest the left foot in the ultra-narrow pedal box. By 1989 cockpits were generally so tightly moulded around the driver that a bulge was necessary to clear the gear lever. This cramped accommodation and the wheelbase and weight distribution problems posed by the new foot position constraint put tall drivers at a distinct disadvantage. For example, the Murray McLarens could not be driven by drivers taller than Prost and Senna. Murray told Staniforth: 'There are certain parameters you cannot alter; fuel capacity, size and weight of the driver, and so forth. If we lost Prost it would mean a new car. It is tailored to him to half an inch everywhere.'

Stiff springing and cramped accommodation do not make for driver comfort. Writing in *Autosport* (March 30

1989), Nigel Roebuck called it 'the era of the compressed driver', commenting, 'I watched some of them struggling aboard and thought of those hideous cages in *Bridge Over the River Kwai* in which the Japanese punished prisoners in the war. They were designed to allow a man to neither sit nor stand.'

Roebuck went on to recount a meeting with Derek Warwick, driver of an Arrows A11. 'Warwick was hobbling around. "I've got three toenails absolutely black and starting to come off." Why? I asked. "Well, I'm having to wear boots a size smaller than I need," Derek replied, "otherwise I can't operate the pedals...

"The car is comfortable in the pit road. It's only when you get out there that the restrictions become obvious. I've got huge bruises on both knees because they are jammed up against the bulkhead."'

Warwick's team-mate Eddie Cheever was a taller driver, and he had trouble vacating his car quickly enough in the mandatory five-second exit test. Cheever remarked to Roebuck: 'You'd have a hard job telling the designer that a two percent loss on the aerodynamic package is worth it for the driver to be comfortable. And I understand that. I don't blame Ross [Brawn – the Arrows designer] at all... I think the regulations are a joke. I'm having a hard time in there, I admit it. I can't move my feet and my knees are just stuck to the bulkead – so if you're about to hit something head on, you can do nothing. You don't have the room to draw your legs back.'

As Roebuck pointed out, the physical toll became obvious to observers after Cheever was spun out on lap 38: 'he is a strong fellow, renowned for his fitness, but 38 laps of acute discomfort in great heat had taken their toll. As he walked away from his car his legs folded under him...'

Discomfort leads to increased fatigue, which in turn makes an accident more likely. Jackie Stewart drove the '88 March in a test session and reported to Roebuck: 'I could hardly have been more impressed, but the cockpit appalled me! I couldn't believe how uncomfortable it was. OK, in a race you are concentrating on racing, I appreciate that, and I admit I had an absolute thing about the cockpits of my cars – everything had to be just right. But the main reason for that was that I knew I functioned far better when I was comfortable. I mean, it's bad enough having a poor driving position in a road car, but in one of these it's

A sturdy roll hoop with proper bracing. The car is a McLaren M23 of early Seventies vintage.

much more important. If a driver is uncomfortable, I maintain that he won't work – can't work – at anything like his maximum efficiency.'

As these words were written, FISA was finalising future regulations setting minimum cockpit dimensions. Even in a more accommodating car, the driver is subjected to a certain amount of discomfort, as Stewart points out in his book, *Principles of Performance Driving*: 'Racing drivers tend to get congested in their upper body. When they recline in a single-seated racing car, muscle tension is involved for considerable periods of time and has a way of tightening and knotting everything up, specifically the shoulders and around the neck. Wearing a crash helmet is a heavy weight to carry, which is exaggerated by the G-forces which drivers experience – whether it be the head going forward under braking or backwards under acceleration, or lateral forces in cornering. In addition to all of that you've got the jolts, the bangs and the bumps due to undulations on the circuit. So, the neck has to go through quite a lot.

'Then you have to consider the central nervous system which extends from the brain through the neck and down through the spine – which is not all that well supported in the case of a racing driver, certainly not in any padded form. He is usually lying in a fibreglass seat, strapped in with his vertebrae sometimes chafing against that seat. So there's not a great deal in the way of body comfort: you're not being very sympathetic to your body when you're driving a racing car.'

Practical means of helping the driver do his job in a more comfortable manner are discussed in the 'Cockpit' section. Here we are concerned with the overall package, and it is clear that a single central fuel tank has a lot to recommend it. Keeping feet behind the front wheel axis is a good thing, but more important is the overall concept of a survival cell. Clearly, though, the regulations for a specific category will have the major bearing on how the cars evolve.

Formula One cars like the other major single seater categories are required to pass a crash test before they are permitted to compete. Group C at the time of writing does not require such a test. Nigel Stroud, designer of a number of Group C chassis including the Mazda 767 and the Richard Lloyd Racing Porsche 962 expressed concern about some designs of Prototype chassis.

'In a side impact one wheel will be pushed back into the side pod which can compromise the strength of the monocoque if a front impact follows. Any car with side-mounted radiators is particularly vulnerable as the monocoque is usually shallower and therefore less rigid.'

Since January 1 1982 it has been obligatory for Grand Prix cars to contain a so-called survival cell, in other words a protective structure surrounding the driver. This cell is intended to provide full impact protection, extending from ahead of the soles of the feet to behind the seat. The mandatory structure is required to be made from panels of composite material with a honeycomb core of a crush-resistant nature. Regulations specify minimum dimensions for the height and width of the survival cell and require the provision of an integral headrest.

Given the survival cell and likewise mandatory twin roll-over structures fore and aft of the driver, the modern Grand Prix car is an inherently stronger and safer machine than any of its predecessors. Further, advances in the design and production of composite materials has brought about major improvement in driver safety as well performance through dramatically increased chassis strength and rigidity.

The use of aluminium honeycomb composite panels in chassis construction was pioneered by Ford in the mid-Sixties. The experimental 'J-car's monocoque was made from bonded and riveted honeycomb panels. A further developed version of this was the GT40 Mark IV which won at Le Mans in 1967.

In 1966 McLaren built a Formula One monocoque from a composite material called Mallite in which aluminium panels sandwiched a layer of end grain balsa. The Mallite monocoque car was abandoned after a season of disastrous engine reliability and McLaren returned to a conventional sheet aluminium monocoque for logistical reasons. However, the advantage of the more rigid Mallite monocoque had been evident in excellent slow corner performance.

Aluminium honeycomb appeared intermittently throughout the late Sixties and early Seventies in Formula One. McLaren used it extensively in the tub of its 1976 M26 design while Harvey Postlethwaite's 1978 design for the Wolf WR3 ground effect car featured a tub formed from a single folded sheet of honeycomb.

Honeycomb material offers excellent protection as each

cell within the honeycomb acts as an individual shock absorber, offering the same resistance to deformation and damage as its neighbour. With plain sheet metal damage would be accentuated by the material's lower rigidity with buckling and folding occurring more easily.

The imposition of the survival cell regulations made composites obligatory and helped spark a revolution in monocoque construction methods. Advanced composites had first appeared in Formula One during the mid Seventies, Hesketh and Hill using aerofoil parts made from carbonfibre composite. Some teams experimented with its use in other areas but it was Peter Wright at Lotus and John Barnard, then of McLaren International, who raised the ante by producing monocoques, for the the 1981 season, which were constructed almost entirely from advanced composites. Soon after Alfa Romeo appeared with a similarly advanced tub, heralding a wind of change that was to blow through Formula One in the next few years.

Within a short time carbon fibre and Kevlar honeycomb-based panels were a common sight in the Grand Prix paddock. Any doubts about the safety of the new materials were quickly dispelled almost singlehandedly by McLaren driver Andrea de Cesaris, who put the McLaren MP4 through a rigorous (albeit unintentional) crash test programme.

By the mid-Eighties carbon fibre monocoques were the Grand Prix norm and had filtered down to the lower reaches of the sport. Carbon fibre and Kevlar bodywork also replaced the once ubiquitous glass fibre on production racing machines.

The introduction of regulation crash testing of sample monocoques in the major single seater racing categories increased safety awareness in the late Eighties. During the late Seventies the tendency to locate a single fuel cell behind the cockpit led to the driver being seated further forward in the chassis until his feet were ahead of the front wheels. Mercifully there were few injuries resulting from this, as designers took extra care to reinforce the forward area, or 'footbox', of the monocoque. A regulation change requiring the positioning of the driver's feet behind the front axle line was introduced in the late Eighties, along with crash testing. A monocoque was then required to withstand a frontal impact of 750 kg at 32m.p.h. without the resultant damage reaching the area of the driver's feet or causing deformation of the pedals.

Since the introduction of composite technology into chassis building, it has emerged that the inherent rigidity of a monocoque tub constructed from such material ensures that impact damage remains localised. The chassis retains its original shape, affording the driver greater protection than a conventional sheet metal tub.

However, praise for the qualities of composite materials should be tempered with caution, as experience has given rise to some drawbacks in their use. Carbon fibre and Kevlar laminates, although extremely strong and rigid, have a weakness in that the stiffness of the two materials is different and can give rise to laminar separation under heavy loads such as impact. Further doubts have been raised as to the ability of Kevlar to resist multiple impacts without breaking down.

Further, Dr. Rowland Cottingham, a motorsports medical officer, writing in *Autosport* in September 1986, raised the following point:

'There is a further extremely worrying and rarely mentioned shortcoming of Kevlar arising from its very strength; it is resistant to all tools currently deployed on rescue units.

'Motor racing safety experts are not the only people very concerned about this material for it is widely used in aircraft fuselages and even professional fire services are unable to penetrate it. Paradoxically, there is one very easy way to destroy it: Kevlar burns very easily.'

The carbon-carbon clutch arrived in the late Eighties and offered instant response with less weight.

Clutch

Although clutchless control might well become standard feature of the 21st century Formula One racing car, and is already a novelty of certain World Championship cars in the late Eighties, the majority of competition cars are going to have clutches for a long time yet. Perhaps the most famous racing clutch is the AP Racing $7\frac{1}{4}$" twin plate unit that achieved so much success with the Cosworth DFV 3.0 litre Grand Prix engine. It was a diaphragm spring unit with gear driven $7\frac{1}{4}$" diameter pressure plates and was bolted to a steel flywheel no larger than its outside diameter – just under $8\frac{1}{2}$". The pressure plates were also steel and worked in conjunction with steel driven plates onto which a bronze-based friction material was sintered.

Surprisingly, the turbocharged Formula One era did not call for a triple plate version of the AP clutch, in spite of spiralling torque. AP merely found it necessary to thicken up the pressure plates. With greater vibration and harsher power characteristics it also became necessary to introduce a 12 rather than 6 bolt flywheel attachment for certain engines. However, some weight was pared off by a switch from pressed steel to aluminium cover. In 1986 AP Racing rightly received a British Design Council Award in recognition of the excellence of its classic clutch.

The late Eighties brought two important Formula One developments: the introduction of the $5\frac{1}{2}$" lug driven clutch and the arrival of carbon-carbon as a friction material. The switch to a smaller clutch was pioneered by the Honda-Ralt Formula Two team in the mid Eighties and offered the twin benefits of a potentially lower crankshaft axis and a smaller mass. Since the smaller mass was concentrated near the centre of the crankshaft axis there was less inertia. That in turn offers, in theory, superior engine response and better acceleration, and should also make for faster gearchanging.

The advent of the carbon-carbon clutch was even more significant from the point of view of the driver. Carbon-carbon clutches followed the development of carbon-carbon brakes, employing a similar carbon/graphite material (as described in the brake sections). AP first tried

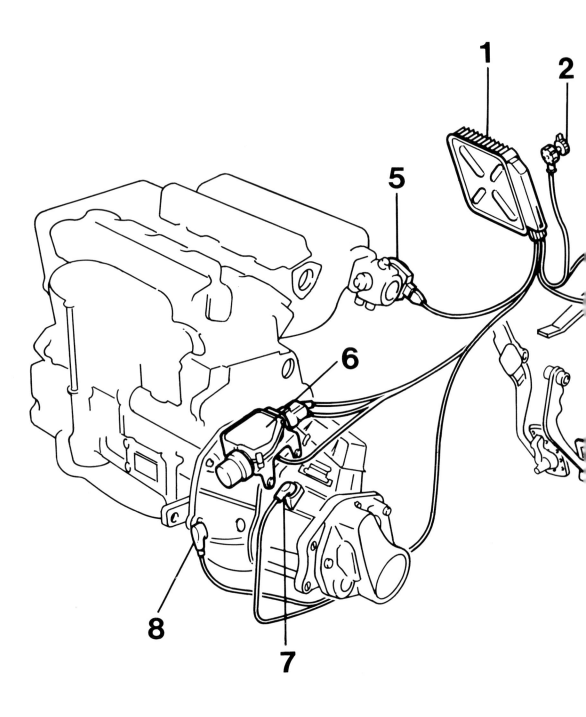

a carbon-carbon clutch in the DFV era, converting a regular twin plate 7¼" unit, working with material supplied by the American Hitco company. Since it was not practical to make the carbon-carbon plates as thin as the items replaced, a single plate unit emerged. It didn't work well and AP suggested that Hitco should improve the low temperature co-efficient of friction of its material, as the clutch slipped badly when cold.

Hitco solved the problem but AP found itself too busy with the demands of the turbo era to continue development and it was left to Hitco neighbour Tilton Engineering to continue the project in the USA. Away from the Formula One rat race McLane 'Mac' Tilton – AP's major West Coast distributor – set ex-AP engineer John Lindo on the project and he soon had a clutch working in a heavy stock car. Hitco had developed a material with stable friction properties at temperatures as low as 212 degrees centigrade, and it was found that only a small input of heat was necessary to double the co-efficient of friction. A conventional clutch had a mu value of around 0.3. Lindo's clutch had a static value of 0.2 which rose rapidly to 0.4.

By 1986 the 7¼" gear driven clutch developed by Lindo was working in a wide variety of American racing cars and at the end of the year Tilton signed a formal agreement to manufacture clutches from carbon-carbon blanks supplied by Hitco. Tilton points to a number of advantages of the carbon-carbon clutch, not least significantly reduced weight and inertia. He says even more mass is often saved in the flywheel, by manufacture in aluminium rather than steel, than in the clutch itself. Marginal engine performance and fuel economy gains result. Further, Tilton offers that carbon-carbon plates won't warp so release cleanly and dampen vibrations. After initial burnishing the wear rate falls rapidly and the clutch should last far longer than a conventional clutch in most applications. It can also withstand standing starts better and can be slipped intentionally without adverse affect, allowing a driver to make up for having the wrong gear, as when baulked in a slow corner. Up to a point heat is beneficial to the carbon-carbon clutch since it increases rather than decreases the co-efficient of friction. Clearly the carbon-carbon clutch is a 'driver friendly' device.

In January 1987 Lotus requested a 5½" lug driven version directly to replace the conventional AP item it was running on its Honda V6 engine. A 1.5 kg. three-plate

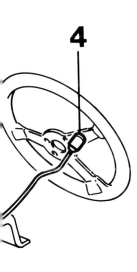

Lancia's system: 1 - ECU; 2 - programme selector; 3 - gear lever direction sensor; 4 - override; 5 - fuel inlet valve sensor; 6 - activator; 7 - gearbox sensor; 8 - r.p.m. sensor.

carbon-carbon clutch duly replaced the regular 3.6 kg. 5½" clutch and this was good enough to claim pole at Monaco and win Detroit. Tilton admits that elsewhere race winner Senna often used a conventional clutch on race day as he found the carbon-carbon item insufficiently 'aggressive' at the start. On the other hand, Ferrari also adopted the Tilton clutch and its drivers Alboreto and Berger apparently found it 'too aggressive'.

AP introduced its own carbon-carbon clutch in 1987, stirred by Tilton's progress, using material supplied by the French Carbone Industrie concern. AP started with a four plate 5½" lug driven clutch and soon found it could take the fourth plate out. The AP clutch was introduced at Monza with the Honda-Williams team, and won. In 1988 AP Racing took over the Formula One market from Tilton, exploiting its existing trackside clutch and brake service facility which Tilton was not in a position to match. A much smaller company, Tilton Engineering did, however, manage to keep a toe in the water and introduced a smaller release bearing for a 5.0:1 rather than 3.5:1 ratio to eliminate the 'switch effect' of the carbon-carbon clutch. Tilton also expanded into the Indy Car market with the same 5½" clutch, though for 1990 carbon-carbon clutches were due to be banned as part of a general clamp down on the use of composite materials in the transaxle and suspension.

Expense was the reason cited by the Indy Car authorities for the planned advanced composite ban, but at the time of writing Tilton was in the process of making an appeal against the exclusion of the composite material clutch on the grounds that a higher purchase price was typically offset by longer life. Mac Tilton points out that the Shierson and Simon Indy Car teams both managed to run a Tilton clutch for the entire season in '88.

Longevity was a feature of clutches run by American Camel Lights prototypes. Indeed, Jim Downing managed to run the same clutch for three seasons in his Mazda propelled Argo. Tilton gained wide acceptance among Camel Lights runners but the bigger GTP cars did not find such success. With high power, high torque and high weight GTP teams found unacceptably high wear rates. For example, both Electramotive Nissan and TWR Jaguar toyed with carbon-carbon clutches in '88 without success. However, at the time of writing Tilton was confident of finding an answer to the challenge of the potent 900kg.

machine, and AP Racing was also addressing the problem.

Regardless of the type fitted, carbon-carbon or metal, the competition clutch is invariably hydraulically operated with the pressure controlled by the pedal ratio and the relative sizes of master and slave cylinders. The actual hydraulic system is straightforward and, provided quality components are employed, should be reasonably trouble-free. It is worth running a positive mechanical stop in the system to avoid wasting time and reliability overstressing the diaphragm. There should also be a rest for the left foot – if there is room for it – since riding a clutch is a sure way to abuse it.

Shifting without the clutch can be an effective way of abusing a gearbox. However, if the driver can synchronize engine r.p.m. properly he will be able to shift a dog-engagement type 'box without the clutch and without gearbox damage. That won't save time but will save a foot movement. It is easier said than done and proper clutchless transmission systems have long been a goal of racing car designers. The two pedal system clearly improves brake and throttle control, as well as saving the foot movement from one pedal to another. In particular two pedal control allows the driver to concentrate on careful modulation of the brake pedal for maximum retardation.

The first mid engine racing car with clutchless control was Jim Hall's innovative Chaparral 2 way back in the mid Sixties. This series of Can Am and World Championship sports cars employed a so called 'automatic' gearbox supplied by General Motors, with whom Hall had a close working relationship. In fact, the GM transmission was worked by a conventional gear lever and incorporated a conventional enough dog-engagement two – later three – speed gearbox. However, rather than employing a clutch the gearbox was fed through a hydraulic coupling. This provided progessively reducing slip, and it locked up rigidly at something in the region of 5,000r.p.m. The driver eased the throttle to unload the dogs then snatched the next gear as quickly as possible. The fluid coupling absorbed shock loads and lessened any tendency for the rear wheels to lock under harsh use of engine braking.

Lotus toyed with a semi-automatic clutch on its mid Seventies Formula One car, an AP development. The idea was that the clutch pedal should be replaced by a button on the gear lever, allowing proper two pedal control. The button operated a solenoid which in turn admitted pressurised hydraulic fluid to the clutch slave cylinder. Thus, holding the button down left the clutch disengaged. Clearly it was necessary to incorporate a pump to maintain the fluid at high pressure and this was worked off the Cosworth DFV starter motor. High pressure fluid was stored in an accumulator, with a sensor to monitor the pressure. The pump was driven by the starter motor running in reverse (so that it did not throw the starter dog into engagement with the starter ring on the engine) and that operation was automatically activated via an additional solenoid whenever the sensor recorded insufficient fluid pressure in the accumulator.

Initial testing was carried out in February 1973 and it was found that the clutch action was too sharp for starting and too sharp on downward changes. Thus, a normal clutch pedal operation was introduced for starting, and this was employed together with a forked brake pedal for operation by either foot. To overcome the problem of downchanges, an extra valve was fitted to restrict the rate of fluid return whenever the brake pedal was depressed. Placed in the fluid return line, the new valve was sensitive to brake pressure.

Ferrari tried a similar system but the concept of an electro-hydraulic clutch suffered from development problems until the advent of on-board micro-computer control systems. That was the key that unlocked the door to fully workable clutchless control systems. Ferrari pioneered a semi-automatic Formula One gearbox that dispensed with both clutch and the gear lever. Instead, the driver had two buttons on the steering wheel: one for up shifts, the other for down shifts, and Mansell won first time out with the system, at Rio. This and the Porsche clutchless, push button gear selector control system, as employed in Group C, are described in the Gear Shift section. Porsche and Ferrari retained a clutch for getting off the line but thereafter its Eighties semi-automatic transmission was clutchless and a driver's dream.

While the likes of Porsche and Ferrari developed semi-automatic, clutchless gear shifting, Lancia developed an automatic clutch, for use with a conventional gearbox, thus going one step beyond the AP/Lotus concept. The work was done in conjunction with the Valeo company and the electronically managed clutch was used on the highly successful Group A Delta which at the time of

*Cockpit of the
Lancia Delta with
electronically
managed clutch.
The clutch can be
manually operated.*

writing (mid '89) was busy dominating World Championship rallies.

The Delta was fitted with a conventional clutch and lever-operated gearbox but just throttle and brake pedal control, while the clutch was operated automatically by electro-mechanical control. The electro-mechanical actuator was activated by pulses sent out by an electronic control unit (ECU). Fully programmed, the ECU took readings from a variety of sensors before determining the manner in which the clutch should be operated since many factors affect how it should be engaged or disengaged – road speed, engine revs, up or down change, road surface condition and so forth.

The Lancia-Valeo competition clutch had sensors for gear lever direction, engine r.p.m., gearbox primary shaft r.p.m., fuel inlet valve position and engaged gear position, plus a handbrake sensor. The ECU's decision-making process was further refined by a switch which allowed the driver to chose between alternative programmes according to surface conditions (so that, for example, engagement will not be so rapid on ice as to induce wheelspin). In addition, the driver had an over-ride push-button to allow the clutch to be engaged or disengaged manually if necessary.

From rest, the first tiny movement of the gear lever is detected and the clutch is dis-engaged. As soon as the gears are in mesh the unit is ready to re-engage but it will not do so until the engine speed reaches 1,200r.p.m. And the speed of clutch engagement is directly proportional to the opening angle of the fuel inlet valve so that a slow take off will not lead to an embarrassing stall through sharp clutch action. Clearly, at the start of a special stage the driver will want to rev the engine above 1,200 r.p.m. for a fast getaway and the over-ride button positioned on the steering wheel enables him to do this. He can depress the button, rev the engine as much as he wishes, then let go of the button the instant the flag drops. Speed of re-engagement will then depend upon the road grip available. The handbrake sensor tells the ECU when the driver is attempting a handbrake turn and the clutch disengages momentarily to allow the rear wheels to lock!

Overall, Lancia rally drivers found the two pedal control system an enormous advantage, lessening the effort of driving, allowing faster gear changes and reducing stress on transmission components to boot.

Lancia summarised the advantages of the system for rallying as follows:
- top acceleration from a standing start and no chance of error;
- optimisation of gear change timing;
- less stress of transmission parts;
- easier, two pedal driving (the driver can develop a special technique, operating throttle and brake simultaneously);
- less tiring for the driver who no longer has to think about using the clutch.

The Lancia/Valeo System looks the way ahead for clutch control in competition and everyday motoring.

Cockpit Cooling

In general no provision is made for ventilation on single seater cars except perhaps in conditions of extreme heat. In the past at Grand Prix races run in hot conditions all manner of extra ducting could be seen tacked onto cars. But as aerodynamics became ever more critical the tendency grew to leave the driver to fend for himself. The introduction of the cool suit was no doubt welcomed by many drivers with great relief (see relevant section).

Given a straight choice, a Sports-Prototype manufacturer will logically opt for a spyder rather than a coupé body. The open spyder has the obvious advantages of reduced frontal area and reduced weight. Further, it offers better visibility for the driver, as well as better ventilation and a less claustrophobic cockpit. The only advantages of the coupé are better streamlining and better driver protection in inclement weather. Streamlining is only a major consideration at Le Mans, where the unique three and a half mile long Mulsanne straight puts the emphasis on drag rather than downforce. However, drag is a product of frontal area as well as a non-dimensional drag coefficient, so the question of streamlining is not clear cut. There were just a few coupé projects at Le Mans during the spyder years of the Seventies. However, in 1978 the winning Renault Alpine spyder was fitted with a hinged cockpit 'bubble' of clear perspex for improved streamlining which upped Mulsanne speed. There was a slot in the front of the canopy for improved forward vision and ventilation, yet the drivers complained of excessive cockpit heat.

In Group C and GTP the widespread use of turbocharged engines which generate tremendous amounts of heat make ventilation and cooling an important consideration for the chassis designer.

Group C and GTP car regulations demand a minimum windscreen height and the enclosure of all mechanical components by the coachwork. In the Sixties there was a comparable minimum windscreen height for homologated sports-racing cars but constructors were free to run without a roof panel over the cockpit. Ferrari toyed with both 'coupé' and 'spyder' versions of its fabulous 512

Cockpit of the 1989 Aston Martin Group C car showing cockpit cooling vents in dash.

model, the latter essentially a coupé without a cockpit roof panel.

Removing the cockpit roof saved some weight and allowed a carefully-shaped roll bar to help direct air towards the spoiler (this was the time before the general use of rear wings). However, any aerodynamic gain was minimal. The main gain was a saving in the region of 25kg. and in practice any difference in performance between the spyder and coupé versions was marginal. 'Sometimes a driver couldn't tell any difference at all', designer Mauro Forghieri told the author. He says the use of either often came down to driver preference – the spyder was easier to get in and out of and some drivers liked the open roof. But in the wet there was no such choice – 'the spyder was terrible in the rain!'

Drivers tend to complain of lack of ventilation in fine conditions but complain of too much in wet weather and sometimes ventilation is too good and a car becomes flooded!

But we digress. In the Group C/GTP era fully enclosed cockpits are the order of the day and cockpit cooling is a major concern. An over-heated driver is likely to be a tired, exhausted driver and certainly will not perform as well as a cool driver. The adverse effect of the drag caused by cooling ducts is insignificant compared to the potential gain in driver performance.

This was underlined at Jarama in the 1989 World Sports-Prototype Championship race. Johnny Dumfries lost his Toyota partner for the 300-mile, three and a half hour race on a sinuous course in sizzling 100 degree Farenheit heat. Few expected Dumfries to last the distance, but he did, finishing tenth overall. It was a real feat of stamina and, significantly, Dumfries told *Autosport*: 'I wasn't unduly concerned, because although we don't have cool suits, the ventilation is good in the car'.

Nigel Stroud, designer of the Mazda GTP, says: 'build up of heat is more of a problem than ventilation. We can get a lot of air into the car but it can still be uncomfortable as the exit and changing of air is difficult. To get a really good temperature it would probably be necessary to compromise the aerodynamics. What is really needed is air conditioning. Direct ventilation feeds air in at a very high force'.

The problem of good cockpit ventilation has, of course, been around for a very long time and was particularly

Nose duct of Group C Spice takes in air for cockpit cooling. It's then ducted as shown overleaf...

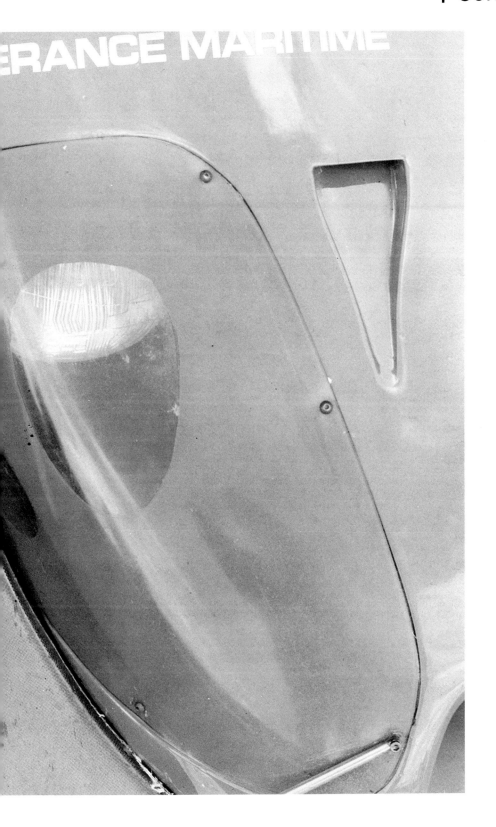

The air travel
through the nose
panel, as far as thi
exit point . .

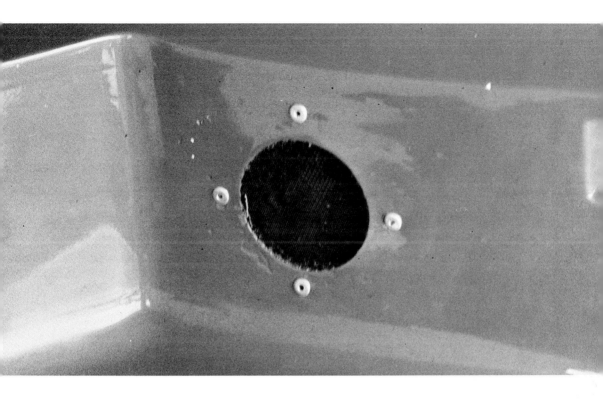

.. which connects with this filtered intake on the front of the tub. From here the air travels to a dash outlet.

acute in the case of the early Porsche 917, which makes an informative case study.

Unveiled in 1969, the Typ 917 had a long, air cooled 180 degree V12 engine yet retained the traditional short wheelbase employed for Porsche's six-cylinder boxer-engined cars. That set the driver well forward in a fully enclosed, low drag coupé chassis. His feet were positioned between the front wheels and their attendant hot brake discs. In the nose was a generous oil radiator which played an important role in the cooling of the 4.5 litre engine.

Oil was circulated between the engine and radiator through chassis tubes (the car of multi-tubular frame construction) while three-into-one exhausts exited at the sides, ahead of the rear wheels. The engine bay was completely closed other than for rearward-facing slots through which the horizontal engine fan drew in air. Air pushed down over the cylinders by the fan was left to escape as best it could through the rear of the car, under a tail section that concealed all mechanical components. The driver was separated from the hot engine bay by a thin sheet aluminium firewall, the fuel sitting alongside him in side sponsons.

Porsche did not overlook the fact that its new 500 b.h.p. projectile was likely to be hot in the cockpit and ducted cooling air from small NACA inlets in the nose, these flanking the oil radiator intake. Nevertheless, the cockpit proved so unbearably hot that Porsche had to supply cool suits for its drivers, these adding the weight of a sizeable ice box.

The Porsche driver cooling problem was not properly resolved until the arrival of the 917K for the 1970 season. This had a re-routed exhaust system which exited out of the back of the car, a system that had been tricky to devise due to lack of space under the horizontally opposed engine. Equally as significant from a cooling point of view was the removal of rear end bodywork: the tail panel was cut away, as was the section immediately above the engine. At last the heat could escape and a cooler driver was not the only advantage – the reduction in engine bay temperature greatly assisted mechanical durability.

More recently, take the case of the Jaguar XJR-6, the car TWR built to restore Le Mans prestige for the Coventry marque. The XJR-6 marked TWR's progression from production to prototype racing team and was rush produced in early 1986, which left chassis designer Tony Southgate little time for detail design. The car carried a nose radiator for reasons of weight distribution and aerodynamic form. The disadvantage of such an arrangement from the point of view of driver comfort is great since a nose radiator leaves a lot of hot air in its wake. This, logically, has to be ducted out through the top of the nose and over the windscreen and it was found that the entire airflow over the central superstructure was consequently at high temperature.

The XJR-6 rolled out without cockpit cooling vents due to the lack of time for such niceties at the design and prototype build stage. At first the team tried picking up air from under the radiator inlet. Often, the most effective place to duct cooling air into the cockpit is at the driver's feet. However, TWR found more success taking air from a NACA duct in the horizontal section of the driver's door. This air was then directed towards the driver's chest and a handy flap allowed him to control the flow.

That was the solution for the XJR-6. It was not ideal. In 1987 the team introduced the refined XJR-8 which boasted a host of improved details. One such improve-

Distinctive cockpit cooling air intake for the 1989 Sauber-Mercedes Group C car.

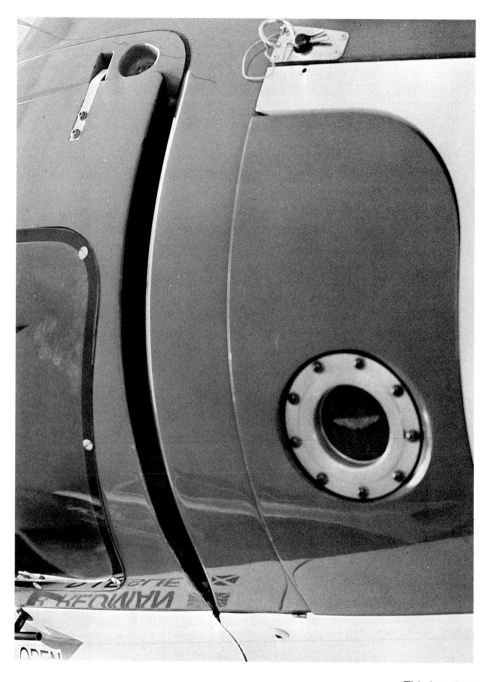

This is not an illfitting door. The gap is left to allow air to escape in the interest of cockpit through-ventilation.

ment was driver cooling. A slim central air intake was incorporated into the nose section ahead of the radiator exit and the cool air collected by this was ducted to two dashboard vents that pointed at the driver's chest. At the rear of the cockpit was a small central roof indent which formed part of a modified engine air intake. A cockpit air exit bled air into this high pressure engine intake, ensuring a good through-flow of air. Such a through-flow was found particularly important to the proper functioning of the cockpit cooling system.

At the Dijon Group C race early in 1989, the Nissan team experienced a spate of problems with the windscreen of its Group C car popping out of its frame. Keith Greene later explained that the car had previously run in testing for 7000 kilometres without a problem. At Dijon a small air duct was added to feed air into the cockpit and this tipped the fine pressure balance within the cockpit and literally blew the screen out! The problem was eventually fixed via a strengthened screen mounting.

Aston Martin also encountered ventilation problems at Dijon and subsequently added an intake over the middle of the splitter, thus ducting air to variable direction vents in the cockpit. The problem of exiting the air from the cockpit was solved by having a tall slot on the trailing edge of each door, which made it appear that the door was not properly closed!

Cockpit Ergonomics

'I hope to be back early from the office'. Bob Wollek prepares for another brilliant stint in his Le Mans Lancia.

The cockpit is the racing driver's office and, as with all working environments, it must be comfortable and conducive to concentration. Clearly it must also be safe, and the question of driver protection is considered at length in the "Chassis" section. We are dealing here with the problem of accommodating the driver well within a proper survival cell, a feature that should be designed and built into the chassis of all competition cars. Where that is not feasible there must at least be a full roll cage, and there is a separate section devoted to roll cage technology.

Indeed, seats and seat belts are also considered separately, as are the steering system, the gear shift, the instrumentation, the brakes, clutch and throttle, the windscreen, even the cockpit cooling system and the provision of fire extinguishing and life support systems. The chassis section considers the basic packaging: we are concerned here as to how all the various elements can be fitted around a driver so that he might best be able to do his job. Ergonomics is the word that springs to mind. Ergonomics is 'the scientific study of man in his working environment.'

A word first on the subject of cockpit padding. Padding is not required on materials that can absorb energy, such as g.r.p., but high density foam protection should be used elsewhere to cushion any blow. It should be appreciated that impact loads can hit a peak – albeit for a matter of milliseconds only – at least as high as 20 g, maybe as high as 50 g. Extreme impact force is survivable if the load is spread over the body. However, it can cause the body to stretch as much as 10%, which means height can grow significantly, while seat harnesses will also stretch. Thus, even with the harness doing its job of keeping the driver in the seat, the driver's body can still contact parts of the car that are up to a good few inches away from him when he is seated normally.

As we have seen, aerodynamic dictates saw the cockpit of late Eighties Formula One cars increasingly cramped as the designers strove to reduce the cross-sectional areas of the fuselage. Under such pressure drivers conceded space to the designer at the mock-up stage, only to find problems operating the controls, knees and toes rubbing and so forth out on the track. The driver must have sufficient space for movement of his arms, legs and feet. He must also have a sensible steering ratio and pedal pressures and be well braced against cornering forces.

Frank Gardner had a colourful way of putting it: 'if you're uncomfortable in the cockpit, you're being flung around, or the wrong steering ratio's making you arms ache, you are operating at less than 100% and you're being distracted. If you're charging around this circuit worrying more about your feet, your arse or your arms than about what's going on around you then you're a great candidate for joining any accident...'

The question of cockpit comfort can only be determined out on the track. The driver has to fit snugly and become part of the machine. Again, as Gardner put it: 'You balance the car through your backside and the small of your back, and the steering wheel should be an almost incidental thing... you must adjust the controls until you can operate them as you want without using the steering wheel as a purchase, and then with rubber padding in the right places you can wedge yourself down into your beaut little single seater really firmly. You don't want to be wobbling around because this will disguise the rhythm of the car from your senses and it is only when you find the rhythm of the car that you can begin to drive it competitively.'

In other words, a proper seat fitting can improve driver performance. Careful thought must be given to the 'office furniture'. The seat must offer very good lateral support and adequate back support, particularly in the lumber region. Thigh support is important and the seat support should go as high up the back as is feasible to reduce strain of driving by reducing the load on the stomach muscles, and this applies as much to lateral support as to back support, particularly in view of high g forces. Even support of the rib cage under the arms is desirable. The driver must also be able to keep his head upright: modern 'physio-philosophy' rejects the desirability of leaning with the bend.

A high support seat will spread the load over fleshy areas of the driver's body and will not require padding, as Paul van Valkenburgh points out in *RaceCar Engineering and Mechanics*: 'in fact, padding adds practically nothing to impact safety and is likely to obstruct the flow of cooling air to the driver's backside. A series of holes drilled in a rigid seat shell will improve circulation, allow perspiration to escape and reduce weight. Mounting an unpadded seat shell rigidly to the chassis also improves the driver's ability to sense every minute force and motion in the car.'

This fact was made forceably to author Bamsey many years ago when he took the seat padding off his first kart. The 14,000r.p.m. single cylinder two stroke then massaged him relentlessly, causing endless aches the following day, but his lap times dropped remarkably.

The desirability of an unpadded seat in a crash situation has been suggested by Carroll Smith, who theorises that padding may allow the driver's back to clash with a seat firmly attached to a rebounding chassis structure. As Smith says, the unpadded seat that is tailored to an individual ought to be the safest, as well as the most comfortable. Similarly, seating position and control position have to be tailored to the driver. Clearly, the steering wheel must be within easy reach: Jackie Stewart says: 'you should be able to grip the top of the wheel with a clenched fist and a bent arm without having to move your shoulders from the back of the seat rest.'

The arms bent, semi-reclining position was well established for single seater and Sports-Prototype drivers prior to the advent of the Brabham BT55 which set another lay-down trend. The Sixties fully reclined position re-introduced by Gordon Murray was more comfortable for some drivers, though others complained that it pushed the chin against the chest. It did not, as widely predicted when the BT55 was announced, affect the driver's ability to control the steering wheel even though the arms were straighter.

Interestingly, after BT55 designer Murray moved to McLaren (where he oversaw a similar fully reclined seating position for the MP4/4 of 1988) Brabham went back to a more upright position. BT56 designer David North told the author, 'Patrese said he found the semi-reclined position less comfortable but more "aggressive".'

Traditionally, racing and sports-racing cars are commanded with an arms-bent and legs-bent stance with the feet slightly splayed. The slight bending at the knees makes operation of the foot pedals slightly easier and more sensitive. However, maximum effort is produced when the brake leg is out straight. The pedals should be floor rather than pendant mounted since they will then follow the same arc as the foot pivoting about the heel. A heel support is a good idea.

Of course, the driver must be able to press the pedals right to the stops and there should be no danger of him pressing two at once inadvertently, or of his foot slipping off. A pedal pad should carry a highly abrasive pad to avoid any danger of the foot slipping off at a crucial moment.

The brake pedal must be set up so that it cannot swing over-centre otherwise braking performance will be compromised through an altered mechanical ratio. The pedal should be positioned so as to allow the driver to blip the throttle, and to heel and toe. Snatching for the throttle must not affect the driver's control of the brake pedal so very precise relative pedal positions are called for. Sometimes forked brake pedals are employed, setting a pad either side of the steering column. This enables a smoother transition between throttle and brakes but may take up the room required for a clutch foot rest. Such a rest avoids the danger of riding the clutch and helps the driver brace himself.

A knees-bent stance can mean legs coming up to interfere with the steering wheel rim, particularly during cross-hands manoeuvres. In turn the wheel then has to be moved up and it could consequently intrude into the eye line, though this is unlikely. However, a higher position might well dictate a nine- rather than an 11-inch diameter rim and not all drivers are happy with such a small wheel. It is worth remembering that everything ahead of the driver that is above the level of the mouth will intrude badly into the field of vision.

The gear lever hand will want to be about level with the knee and it is important to ensure that there is somewhere for the elbow to go during changes. It should be only a short reach from wheel to gear knob so that the driver's hand falls naturally to the knob. However, adequate clearance must be provided to the wheel in all gears, and for the driver's leg, while the knuckles shouldn't rub on the bodywork during shifts.

Switches should be positioned within easy reach of the driver when he is firmly belted in and must be clearly marked. The ignition kill switch and fire extinguisher control must be readily at hand and the driver should familiarise himself with the operation of them, so that it is second nature. That could be vital in a shunt. The instruments should be close to the driver's line of sight so that he can glance at them and must be clearly visible when the steering wheel is at the normal straight-ahead position without the driver having to move his head. When conventional gauges are employed an upright needle position should indicate a normal operating temperature or pressure. Back-up warning lights are advisable and the total number of instruments should be kept to a minimum.

Wherever possible the driver should be shielded from excessive heat and fumes, and in an open car from buffeting. Buffeting by the air stream can knock a driver's head about – that does his concentration no good at all. Careful windscreen design is called for. Doors must also be designed thoughtfully. All too often aerodynamic forces pull open a door that has inadequate catches. The Le Mans winning Mercedes-Sauber C9 employed a neat door catch – it was taken from the rear hatch of a Renault R5! Good water sealing is another consideration, though door seals are invariably among the first items to go in any weight trimming exercise. If a car is underweight, proper door sealing is worth considering. Sometimes gullwing doors are employed but these are banned in IMSA in view of the danger of a driver getting trapped in an upturned car.

Overall, the cockpit must be functional and cleanly designed, with nothing that can snag on a race suit. Any part that the driver is likely to rub against should be covered so as to minimise abrasion. As we have noted, from the safety standpoint it is essential that any part of the cockpit that the driver's head may contact in a shunt be well padded. A safe headrest is essential and the cockpit should be functional and, as far as possible, free of any protrusions that could injure the driver. A gear lever contacted a driver's helmet in an Eighties Sports-Prototype shunt, illustrating how even an aluminium honeycomb tub (as in this case) can fold up. Any avoidable protrusion that – however unlikely – could hit the driver should be designed out. And, should it come to the worst, the driver must be able to evacuate the cockpit quickly and easily.

If comfort is important, how much does a Grand Prix driver enjoy? Initially drivers complained of lack of comfort in the ultra-narrow 1988 March Formula One car but as the car became quicker the complaints diminished. As Ian Phillips, Manager of the team, observed: 'If the car is quick the driver is comfortable! However, we do take a lot of trouble – within parameters – to ensure comfort'. March tailor-made its cars to fit the driver.

Steve Nichols of McLaren commented: 'Driver comfort is more important than aerodynamics, and it is not necessary to degrade aerodynamics greatly. Cramped cockpits are a product of poor design.'

In the '89 McLaren cockpit there were small amounts of padding to aid comfort, this added during the initial test runs of the car, 'fine tuning' the cockpit.

John Barnard felt that driver comfort was a very important consideration and pointed out that without its automatic gearbox the Ferrari 640 would have necessarily been wider.

Nigel Stroud of Mazdaspeed feels that the lack of driver comfort in a modern racing car is a result, 'not of bad design, rather a lack of design. Driver comfort is usually the last thing on the list for a designer. We should pay more attention to comfort and it could be achieved without detrimental effect.'

The Mazda Group C, Stroud points out, 'was originally designed in Japan for the Japanese physique – high headroom, short legroom – while later examples were changed slightly to accommodate the frame of European drivers.'

Nissan, like most other 1989 Group C teams, had individually moulded seat panels for each driver, whereas rival Mazda had an adjustable seat permanently mounted in the car, which moved backwards and forwards.

Professor Sid Watkins, President of the FISA Medical Commission, interviewed at Monza in September 1989, expressed the view that the design of cockpits on some contemporary Formula One cars was dangerous in that they restricted the exit or removal of the driver. Regulations required that a driver be able to exit his car in five seconds or less.

Eddie Cheever's difficulty in passing that test at the 1989 Brazilian Grand Prix meeting was the cause of concern among officials and subsequently suggestions were made for the implementation of a rule governing the minimum size of the cockpit. Regarding this, Professor Watkins pointed out the difficulty in drawing up legislation in this area: 'a minimum cockpit size that would

accommodate Cheever would have Nakajima rolling around inside'.

Tidy layout of the cockpit of the 1989 Toyota Group C car. Note clear indication of extinguisher and master switch.

Cool Cap and Cool Suit

As noted in the Cockpit Cooling section, Porsche employed cool suits as long ago as the Sixties as a means of combatting excessive coupé cockpit temperatures. In fact, Porsche was not the first to exploit the cool suit concept for one Paul Goldsmith had already developed a system for use in a NASCAR stock car. Goldsmith circulated coolant through a network of arteries incorporated in a special garment that was worn under the driver's overalls.

NASCAR cockpits are notoriously hot. Sports-Prototypes can also be a problem, particularly in hot climes. Porsche at first wanted to exploit a Goldsmith-type system in its low drag coupés to eliminate the aerodynamic drag caused by conventional cooling ducts. The Porsche system first appeared in public on a long tail 907 coupé tested at Daytona in sunny Florida in December 1967 in preparation for the upcoming 24-hour marathon.

Porsche used water circulated through ice as the coolant and the ice was stored in a rectangular bin fitted into the nose. Such a bin was incorporated into all 907s built for the 1968 racing season. An electric pump was employed to pump water through the system, which embraced a special ribbed driver under-garment. An umbilical cord from the under-garment allowed the driver to plug himself into a dashboard connector and there was a control knob to allow him to vary the flow according to his cooling requirement. The drawback was that the ice bin was effective for less than one hour so had to be replenished at each pit stop. And, of course, the ice was extra weight and Porsche was very conscious of weight. Often the system was not employed for that reason.

A contemporary approach to the problem of driver cooling – which can affect single-seater drivers as well as those working in enclosed environments – is the so-called Driver Cooling System developed by Denis Carlson. The system in fact originated at NASA as the cool helmet. This was designed to tackle the problem of helicopter pilots suffering heat exhaustion, a phenomenon that could lead to a wrong split-second decision and con-

The traditional method of driver cooling. These days water can be pumped through a special suit.

sequent accident. NASA was approached when such accidents started becoming frequent during the Vietnam war.

NASA designed a hood-shaped bladder that incorporated hundreds of capillary-like channels through which cooling gell could be pumped. The gell was pumped from a container that was kept refrigerated and it was found that cooling the driver's head kept his whole body cool, since the head is the primary area of heat loss for a human being. NASA tests demonstrated that a liquid-cooled helmet could reduce sweat loss by 60%, and it also offered a lower heart rate. The cooling effect reduced heat exhaustion and kept the pilot mentally alert for a longer period.

Carlson adapted the NASA system in the form of a light cap that could be fitted under a crash helmet and Carlson Technology, based at Farmington Hills, Michigan, introduced the lightweight, expensive but effective Driver Cooling System in 1981. David Hobbs was the pioneer, in Trans Am. Soon it spread to CART and IMSA, later to Group C and Formula One. Williams was the Formula One pioneer, at the searingly hot 1984 Dallas Grand Prix. The track broke up in the heat, many aces hit the wall, but Honda-Williams' pilot Keke Rosberg kept his cool and won the race.

'It is actually incredible how it improves one's ability to concentrate' had been John Fitzpatrick's reaction, and many other drivers would echo that sentiment. Carlson told *Autosport*, 'I see the system as being rather like rain tyres: you take it along to races as part of the kit and use it on hot days.' Carlson tailors his system to fit the requirements of specific cars and has developed cool vests further to assist endurance drivers. He has also developed a control system to enable a driver to adjust the level of cooling: some drivers have complained of being over-cooled!

In mid-1989 FISA instigated restrictions on the use of cool hats and suits in World Championship races in response to the use of freon in certain systems; this gas is considered hazardous. FISA confined driver cooling systems to water and air at atmospheric pressure, thus also outlawing glycol, the gell generally favoured. At the time of writing moves were afoot to get glycol re-instated.

Circulated by an electronic pump, glycol is passed

through a tubular copper coil which is submerged in ice and water within a foam insulated container or capsule. The capsule is frozen outside the car and is mounted in a suitable position away from heat: a monocoque sill is the usually favoured place in a prototype.

McLaren tried using the Carlson system in 1983–84 but incorporating such a system into a Formula One design where every measure possible is taken to reduce weight and car size, was a problem. The system was judged an unnecessary excess and was thus discarded. When the system was used, the capsule was installed in a side pod with the electric pump mounted behind the driver's head, on top of the fuel tank.

Drinking and driving is acceptable on the track, but careful choice of beverage and method of delivery is called for.

Drinks Bottle

In 1983 Doctor Jonathan Palmer investigated the impact of race driving on the human body for the UK monthly magazine *Automobile Sport*. Palmer arranged for Formula Three driver Peter Argetsinger to be monitored for stress and fluid loss during the course of a short race. It was a noticeably cold day and Argetsinger had an undramatic race on an untaxing circuit. Nevertheless, in spite of the low temperature, Argetsinger lost 500mls. of water through perspiration in the 30-minute event. Normally one would expect to perspire that amount over 24 hours in similar conditions. Working conditions in a tropical climate can produce a rate of 8,000mls. over 24 hours – Argetsinger's equivalent was 12,000mls. over 24 hours!

It is generally recognised that water loss is one of the main causes of fatigue for a racing driver working in hot conditions. The effect of working in a single seater in a cool climate is less widely appreciated. Clearly, as Palmer pointed out, it is vital to start a race of any length fully hydrated, which means drinking frequently beforehand. And, obviously, a drink bottle can pay dividends.

Paul van Valkenburgh has suggested that 'water might be provided during pit stops, except for the obstruction of full-coverage helmets and interference with other, more necessary pit chores. The water container will have to be insulated and mounted near the driver. Location of the container and drinking tube can be a problem, to avoid natural siphoning action under hard, horizontal accelerations. If a driver should stop sucking and take a breath at such time, a drastically tilted water could maintain the flow enough to choke him. The container should be more than a 45-degree angle below the driver's mouth.'

The Leyton House March Grand Prix Team has experimented with different on-board drinks systems, including one employing an adapted windscreen washer pump. It was reported that Mauricio Gugelmin's retirement from the 1989 Hungarian Grand Prix was caused by the pump short circuiting the whole electrical system on the car. This was, however, later denied by the team (perhaps to cover embarrassment?). The March system was in fact under-used by the drivers. Team Manager Ian Phillips remarked that at the end of a race it was not unusual to find a completely full drink container: 'the drivers liked the fact that it was there, but most of the time it was not used.'

McLaren has rarely found the need to fit a drink system and in the days of Lauda, Willi Dungl's fitness and diet plans apparently made such a consideration unnecessary. Senna once used a system incorporating a small electric pump and regulator connected to a container of fluid. However, according to his team, it was only to moisten his lips.

In endurance racing a drinks system is clearly a useful option. Some feel that a one-hour stint in a Group C car is manageable without fluid replenishment, while others use various systems. Nissan experimented with pumps, then reverted to the cyclist-type bottle from which the driver sucks the required amount of fluid with no risk to his car's electrics.

While mineral water is an obvious fluid to supply for a driver, special fluids can be, and often are, prescribed by specialists. For example, TWR Jaguar driver Patrick Tambay carries the sports drink Isostar in a tummy pouch. Gatorade-type mineral replacement fluid is a popular option.

The following report, *Heat and Fluid Regulation* by Edward St. Mary, M.D. of the Mercy Hospital, Miami, and Team Internist for the Miami Dolphins and the Dolphins' Head Trainer, Robert Lundy gives further insight into the field of fluid replacement.

'Over 70 million people have joined in the fitness boom, engaging in exertional sports such as running, skiing, tennis, biking, etc. Along with 17 million orthopaedic injuries occurring per year, there is a rising documentation of illness due to heat stress, a preventable illness in all age groups.

Five major heat-related illnesses are recognised. Heat edema, heat syncope, heat cramps, heat exhaustion and heat stroke. The first listed is relatively benign but all should be recognised as a series of continuous events, rather than a separate distinct classification that may occur in the susceptible individual.

We are aware of the various electro-physiologic changes of heat regulation and dissipation. These include the basic involuntary thermo regulatory processes located in the hypothalamus as the central coordinating mechanism controlling the various blood temperature changes during muscular activity.

Of equal importance are the temperature receptors in the skin that react to environmental temperatures. Peripheral sensory affectors transmit our perception of heat and cold. This learned response allows us to add or remove clothing, seek a breeze, shade, fan, etc.

The body, under healthy conditions, is well able to conserve electrolytes and water during stress or exertion. In addition to the brain centre, the sweat glands, adrenal glands and kidneys ordinarily can minimise their deficits in heat exposure.

Unfortunately the race car driver cannot take advantage of the three principles of cooling that involve convection, conduction or radiation. The race car driver's equipment (helmet, face protector, suit and shoes) prevent him from conduction and convection relief. Radiation cannot help the driver with the high environmental temperature around him which would cause him to become more heated. Cockpit temperatures may reach 100 to 140 degrees Farenheit for extended periods of time.

The race car driver, during an event, has an average heart rate from 130 to 200 beats per minute. This is more than just the known tachycardia and blood pressure elevation seen in the anticipating response of a class marathoner before a race. One can only presume that this tachycardia involves continuous production of epinephrine and other catecholamines under stress.

The caution given to all exertional participants in sporting events is to lessen the heat exposure, avoid excessive loss of water and salt and prevent excessive heat storage. The race car driver has none of these methods to help him that are under his personal control.

Fortunately, professional drivers are reportedly in good physical shape. The heat acclimated driver will have a lower skin and body temperature and will produce a more dilute sweat without greater loss of sodium. A training effort of ten days under similar thermal conditions should prepare the driver for this endeavour, in a tropical setting especially.

Relying on thirst is not a reliable indicator of the need for fluids in the running athlete or the race car driver. The thirst mechanism underestimates the fluid requirements for 30 to 60 percent of the actual body needs. The driver is further handicapped because he cannot stop long or frequently enough to replenish those lost fluids. These fluid losses vary from two to eight percent of body weight. A 150lb. driver who would lose 4 percent of body weight will have lost six pounds or three quarts of water from his total body composition during a race.

These widely variable losses can be more clearly estimated by the driver/trainer by measuring nude body weight before and after the event.

Care must be taken when prescribing only water to the driver over a long period of time. Replacement solutions are reported to have their greatest benefits on events lasting over one hour. Therefore, when hypotonic fluids are given in large quantities to athletes in general the resulting solution may cause nausea, diarrhoea, exhaustion, electrocardiographic abnormalities and heart failure. Admittedly, this would be rare in the driver because he just doesn't have the time to consume large quantities of fluid. The elaborate dilutional formulae given in the laboratory for the running athlete therefore cannot but generally apply to the driver because he cannot alter the thermoregulatory processes that surround him.

The most recent report, *Tribune Sports Report*, September 2 1987, quoting Carl V. Gisolfi, PhD., former President of the American College of Sports Medicine, suggests that 'combination of simple sugars or glucose polymers (Gatorade is 4% sucrose, 2% glucose) seem the most effective when ingested during prolonged exercise, they do not adversely affect plasma volume, sweat rate or the rise in core body temperature compared with water.

In the same article, Dr. Gisolfi reported on another revealing study. Subjects were studied in a simulated marathon in 95 degree heat while exercising at 70% of their maximum O_2 uptake. Rectal temperatures rose to 104 degrees Farenheit recorded for two hours with no fluid replacement. Drinking one litre of water thirty minutes before the test made no difference in core temperature, nor did sponging with a wet towel during the tests. However, ingesting 200cc. of warm or cold water every twenty minutes decreased the body core temperature.

Conclusion: athletes in general have the opportunity to adjust their environmental losses of fluid by replenishing their needs on a somewhat demand basis. Race car drivers, by the nature and demands of their sport, are not allowed this privilege.

The most pleasant personal and physiological advice to any athlete, including the race car driver, is to encourage the intake of more cold water plus iced-down replacement solutions for short- and long-term racing respectively, wherever there is that opportunity.'

Ear Defenders

Risk of damage to hearing is a problem for drivers, team personnel, race officials and spectators alike. In fact, anyone coming into close contact with unsilenced racing engines should be aware of the threat. Excessive noise can cause temporary hearing damage, like that experienced after a rock concert. The ears may ring for a few days afterwards but full recovery eventually occurs. However, extended exposure to sources of intense sound, such as racing engines, can cause permanent deafness. The temptation to appear 'macho' by shunning the use of ear plugs or ear defenders is foolish, as the onset of a chronic state of deafness may be detected too late for remedy.

Apart from deafness, excessive noise can be the cause of fatigue and, in extreme cases, nausea and dizziness. Adequate ear protection avoids these hazards. In general the higher the level of motorsport the greater the need for protection. In silenced Production Saloon Car racing and some lesser single-seater categories the need may not be pressing. However, engines used in the major formulae are invariably unsilenced and are more powerful, and high-revving and ear defence becomes vital.

Ear plugs do not completely block out noise, acting instead to reduce overall sound to a bearable level, reducing background sound and voices equally. At excessively high background noise levels tests have shown that the human voice becomes easier to hear if ear protection is worn. Also, with the overall noise reduced, it is easier for the driver and technicians to detect fluctuations in the sound of the engine, perhaps signifying a problem.

Modern ear plugs are made from expanding foam rubber and are compressed before inserting into the ear, expanding when in place. In the past various alternative methods were used including 'glass down' – wads of fine glass fibre – and cotton-wool, which was only really effective if used with a sealant such as petroleum jelly. Another alternative was a rather messy wax compound which was packed into the ear. The foam plug is ideal in that it is comfortable to wear, inexpensive and highly efficient in its protection of the ear. The foam plug is a

Peter Sauber hears only what he wants to hear of the successful Mercedes World Championship bid in '89.

practical proposition for use in a car with an on-board radio system and will reduce the background noise of the engine, making communications more audible. If the foam plug is the obvious choice for a driver, for pit personnel ear defenders of the headphone type are available. A pair of protective domes which completely encircle the ear often double as the headset for a radio/intercom system.

Intercom and radio systems employ headphones which are effective ear defenders.

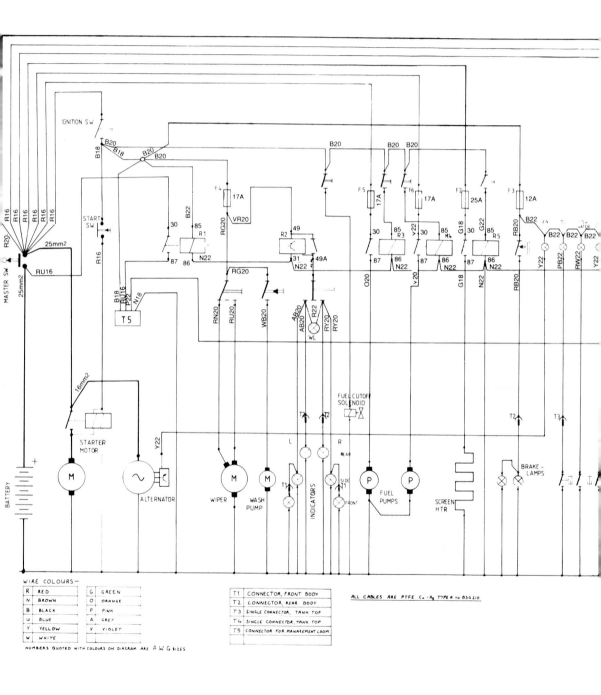

WIRE COLOURS—

R	RED		G	GREEN
N	BROWN		O	ORANGE
B	BLACK		P	PINK
U	BLUE		A	GREY
Y	YELLOW		V	VIOLET
W	WHITE			

NUMBERS QUOTED WITH COLOURS ON DIAGRAM ARE A W G SIZES

T1	CONNECTOR, FRONT BODY
T2	CONNECTOR, REAR BODY
T3	SINGLE CONNECTOR, TANK TOP
T4	SINGLE CONNECTOR, TANK TOP
T5	CONNECTOR FOR MANAGEMENT LOOM

ALL CABLES ARE PTFE Cu-Aℊ TYPE A to BSG210

Electrics

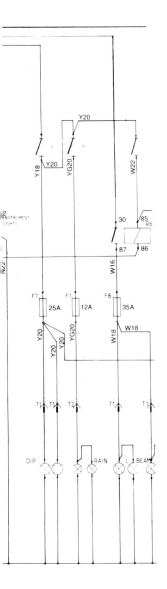

An extract from a wiring diagram for a contemporary Sports-Prototype. Complexity is unavoidable.

It goes without saying that an electrical system should be simplified as far as possible – minimising the field of operation for the dreaded electrical gremlins – and should be carefully produced from high quality components. Too many electrical failures are caused by poor parts and poor preparation. Remember that electricity itself never fails; failure is always mechanical. A faulty connection is typically the culprit. Further, a driver should be fully conversant with his car's system since electrical gremlins have a tendency to strike out on the track, stranding an otherwise healthy machine.

Paul van Valkenburgh sensibly recommends an emergency back-up system. 'The extra wire weighs next to nothing, and even spare coils, amplifiers and voltage regulators could be worth their weight in getting the car back to the pits. The only component that can't be easily backed up is the distributor. Of course, a master shut-off switch is usually required, and it can also fail. Therefore, the duplicate wiring system should begin at the battery, with another normally-off switch in the line. The back-up system doesn't need to pass current to anything more than a fuel pump and the engine – assuming that it can be cut-in before the engine dies and needs restarting'.

It is important to provide an ignition 'kill switch' that the driver can quickly reach. Perhaps the best place is on a horizontal steering wheel spoke so that he can operate it with his thumb without moving his hand. The battery must be securely mounted and enclosed in a proper battery box to avoid sparks or acid spillage, even if it is of the usual 'non-spill' type. Further, all electrical circuits should be encased in fireproof material.

Virtually all governing bodies require an externally accessible master switch which cuts all current from the battery. This isolation switch should be let into the battery earth lead. It will not only cut the ignition but will also ensure that the pumps are shut down. Otherwise, if a fuel line is ruptured the pumps might help fuel a fire. Note that keeping the pumps close to the tank helps block the fuel flow when the electricity is cut. It is clearly a good precaution to have a second master switch within reach of the driver in case help is late in arriving or the driver can anticipate the impact.

The external master switch must be very clearly marked. The switch should be highly visible and straightforward to operate. It sounds obvious, but isn't always the case...

Track marshals complain that due to the lack of standardization in the positioning of the external kill switch, precious seconds can sometimes be spent hunting for it. A recent innovation by some Grand Prix organisers is to circulate a sheet showing the switch position on the competing cars among marshals and track workers. A sensible idea which could be copied at all levels of the sport.

On a current Formula One car it is rare to find a back-up electrical system. The McLaren team considered its '89 electrical system reliable and the extra weight of a back-up system unnecessary. In a world where every gramme of weight is saved where possible, this is a representative view. In prototype racing a back-up system is also generally considered unnecessary, except for Le Mans where the circuit is more than twice the length of any other the teams visit and the event is all about making the finish. It is, however, common to run a back-up system for the fire extinguisher, as Nissan and a number of others do.

Williams-Honda in full battle dress. The electrical master switch on the roll hoop is still easy to spot.

*Fire extinguisher
tucked away in the
engine bay - this is
the 1989 Formula
Three Ralt.*

Fire Extinguishers

Fire extinguishers were traditionally of the CO_2 dry chemical type which had some significant drawbacks for racing. The CO_2 compound was discharged at around minus 100° F, having an adverse freezing effect on human skin, while the dry chemical residue made a mess of the car and engine. Thankfully, Du Pont developed an alternative, Halon 1301 (Bromotrifluoromethane, or BTM) with none of these drawbacks and two to three times the effectiveness on a per-pound basis. Halon 1301 is an inert gas and most fuel and oil will not burn with as little as a four per cent concentration of it in the atmosphere. It is also non-toxic but refills are expensive.

At the 1977 Argentine Grand Prix one drawback of Halon 1301 did emerge. An extinguisher bottle filled with the gas exploded in Mario Andretti's Lotus 78. So fierce was the explosion that it cut brake and oil lines and Andretti was blinded by oil at 160 m.p.h. He received sore eyes from extinguisher discharge but thankfully kept the car under control... The problem was the chemical's sensitivity to heat. As a result, extinguishers using the slightly more toxic Halon 1211 (Bromochlorodifluoromethane or BCF) were introduced and these have become universally adopted in single seater racing. The better ventilation allowed the use of the more toxic chemical: the less toxic Halon 1301 continued to be used in closed cockpit cars, where it is still the norm.

From the point of view of economy and for a quiet life, accidental discharge is clearly to be avoided. A safety pin can be incorporated in the control mechanism while the car is off the track but it must be very obviously tagged so that there is no danger of it being left in place while the car is running. The driver will not have the time to pull a safety pin if he needs his extinguisher system...

In the event of an incident a driver should be prepared to operate his system even in anticipation of impact since the gas will not injure or even disturb him. Waiting until the car has made solid contact might be too late; an unconscious driver cannot help himself. Conversely, the system should not be triggered too soon as the gas will get blown away and used up before the fire breaks out.

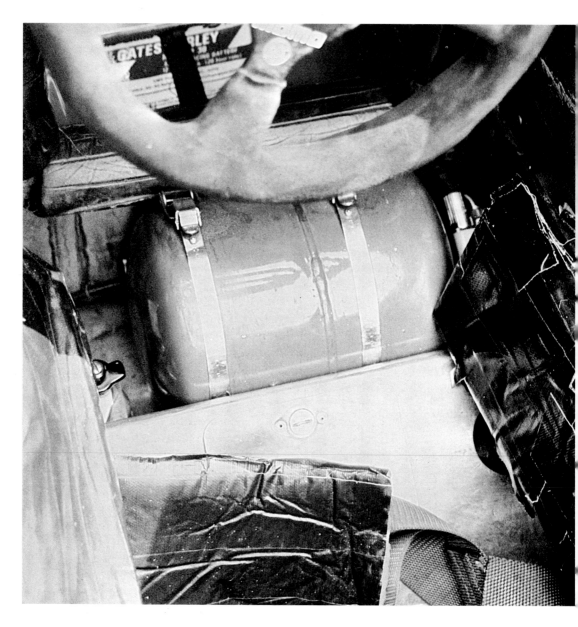

Tucked neatly under the driver's knees is a popular location for the extinguisher bottle.

Heat and inertia sensitive switchgear was experimented with in the early days of onboard extinguisher systems but has now been almost universally discarded. The potential unreliability of such triggers counteracts any advantages. For example, with the dramatic increase in downforce during the ground effect era, designers feared inertia switches could be triggered simply by the G forces generated. Nowadays G forces are scarcely less in the major formulae. In endurance racing the effect on an inertia switch of dropping a newly-refuelled Group C car off its jacks is viewed as another potential problem area. The constant high temperatures generated by turbocharged race engines made the use of heat switches impracticable.

A modern extinguisher system employs steel or aluminium bottles to carry the extinguishant, which is in liquid form and vaporises when discharged. The bottles are mounted on the chassis by metal straps. The bottles should be mounted near enough to the driver so as not to get torn off in an accident: under the knees is a popular and sensible location. However, typically the regulations do not specify location and the bottles are often positioned primarily to help optimise weight distribution.

Steel lines run from the bottles to nozzles that can be mounted anywhere in the car. A mechanical system is operated by a pull cable attached to a pin which punctures a sealing disk to release the chemical. An electronic system is triggered by a switch on the dashboard (this should be in easy reach *and* in sight of the driver) which completes a discharge circuit kept separate from the car's other electrical systems. This ensures that the extinguishers will operate even if the rest of the system is destroyed.

The pull cord or switch must be clearly marked and a dashboard switch should be protected against accidental operation, typically by a plastic surround. Outside the car the location of the trigger mechanism is invariably required by regulation to be clearly marked and should be easily accessible. Even single seaters should have a separate external switch. This switch – a loop or toggle – is typically located on or near the roll-over bar structure, and under FISA regulations has to be marked by a decal with a red letter E in a circle of at least 100mm. diameter.

Choosing the best distribution of nozzles can be difficult. The engine bay, fuel tanks and cockpit are all

Alternative cockpit locations for an extinguisher bottle, in club hillclimb single seaters.

areas worthy of consideration but servicing all three can spread the effect too thinly. Regulations may well enforce a certain distribution. By way of a typical example, the Jaguar XJR-6 Group C car was equipped with two Lifeline bottles, one discharging into the cockpit, the other into the engine trumpets. This was in line with precise FISA regulations governing extinguishing systems on Group C cars. FISA demanded the use of Halon 1301 or 1211 with a 2.5kg bottle discharging for at least 60 seconds into the cockpit (30 seconds in the case of 1211) and a 5kg bottle discharging for at least 10 seconds into the engine.

FISA regulations further stipulated that extinguisher systems equipment must be able to withstand fire, that the nozzles be installed in such a way that they are not pointed directly at the driver (to avoid burns caused by the extreme cold) and that the system be protected against impact. In addition it was mandatory that "each extinguisher bottle be installed in such a way that it is capable of withstanding accelerations of up to 25g, no matter how these are applied.

In terms of triggering the following rule was applied: 'The two systems must be triggered simultaneously. Any triggering system is allowed. However, a source of energy not coming from the main source must be provided in the case of a triggering system which is not exclusively mechanical. The driver seated normally at his steering wheel with his safety harness attached must be able to trigger the system manually; the same applies to any person outside the car. The means of triggering from the exterior must be positioned close to the circuit breaker or combined with it . . . Automatic triggering by heat sensor is recommended. The system must work in any position, even when the car is upside down.'

To this end a system was devised using twin pipes within the extinguisher cannister, tipped with brass spheres that ensured that at least one pipe remained in contact with and thus continued to discharge the extinguishant regardless of the position of the car, even working if it were inverted.

FISA regulations for single-seater categories required the reversal of the Group C arrangement: a 5kg bottle to cover the driver and cockpit, a 2.5kg bottle covering the engine.

Interviewed during 1989, McLaren engineer Steve Nichols expressed the view that inertia and heat switches

E for extinguisher.
Clear indication of
the location of the
external trigger is a
matter of life and
death

are not totally foolproof and could be dangerous if accidentally triggered; an extinguisher discharging into the engine or cockpit when a driver is flat out at around 200 m.p.h. could be catastrophic. He also felt that, given the facilities available at a modern Grand Prix, the car ought to be reached by track workers in a sufficiently short period of time should a fire occur.

For all precautions taken by a team in the area of fire protection, the driver may well need back-up from the track marshals. Unfortunately not all circuits are equipped with inert gas-type extinguishers. Many still rely on dry powder type apparatus. Chemicals used in dry powder extinguishers include sodium bicorbonate, sodium chloride, potassium bicarbonate and amonium phosphate. Although effective at fire control, these leave a powder residue. Careful cleaning and removal of the powder is essential after a car has been sprayed with such an appliance. David Purley's terrible accident at the 1977 British Grand Prix meeting was caused by the throttle slides of his car jamming open due to hardened extinguisher powder after a small engine fire had been put out with a powder extinguisher.

It is a good policy to familiarise course workers with the location of the extinguisher and master switch on your car. This will not only improve your chances of survival, it will help minimise their exposure to fire.

*Eighties Group C
pits fuel rig. Not the
meter - there was a
set allocation per
race.*

Fuel System

A spectacular crash marred the 1964 Indianapolis 500. On the second lap Dave McDonald spun out and hit the concrete retaining wall. The impact ruptured the car's full fuel tanks and seven other cars in the tightly-bunched field became involved in a fiery pile-up. Eddie Sachs died in the melée and McDonald later succumbed to his injuries. Prior to the accident the fire hazard had become somewhat forgotten at the Brickyard, the traditional alcohol fuel far less volatile than the gasoline fuel that Ford had developed its new V8 engine to run on. Subsequently rules were introduced to regulate the handling and storage of fuel in the car and in the pits.

For the 1965 race Firestone developed the in-car 'fuel cell'. Housed inside a metal tank with walls of a regulation minimum width, the cell was a thick rubber bladder which was inserted through a small oval hatch. Once inside the bladder expanded to fill the available space. Its presence greatly increased the rupture resistance of the tank, experience in the aerospace industry showing that a flexible membrane within a rigid fuel tank could survive considerable impact and deformation and would offer resistance to tearing. A Firestone-evolved, low density, sponge-like plastic foam filled the bladder and, being 96% void, caused no significant loss of fuel capacity. The material absorbed fuel as quickly as it was fed into the cell. In the event of an accident in which both tank and cell were damaged, the foam would prevent excessive leakage of fuel, cutting down the flame front should the spillage be ignited, the intensity at which a fuel fire burns being in direct proportion to the flow rate from the ruptured tank.

The new fuel cell was ideal for the innovative chassis structure introduced at this time by Colin Chapman. The monocoque tub essentially consisted of two long hollow tubes connected by bulkheads and a floor panel. Those 'torsion box' tubes were the ideal location for safety cells. The stiff monocoque construction incorporating them marked such a significant step forward in driver safety that regulations were subsequently introduced making the use of monocoque-type construction methods and rubberised fuel tanks mandatory in the major racing

*Waiting for the fuel
stop. This crew
member has the
overflow bottle
ready to plug in.*

formulae.

Further developments in fuel cell design continued apace during the late Sixties and early Seventies. The military aerospace companies showing the way with the evolution of allegedly crash- and bullet-proof fuel tanks. Multi-layered, rubberised nylon walls, coagulant cell wall coatings, laminates of nylon and polyester resin and rubberised Kevlar (a super high-strength fibre used in the manufacture of bullet-proof vests) were developed in the quest for improved cell puncture resistance.

Late in 1971 *Ingenere* Carlo Chiti, then of Autodelta, the competition department of Alfa Romeo, announced a specially designed racing car safety fuel tank. Viewed in cross section the tank was constructed internally of alternating corrugated layers laid in a horizontal lattice forming a series of chambers, one series of which contained fuel, another an extinguishant compound. In the event of an accident the separations between the chambers would break down, rendering the resultant mixture inert. Despite praise and official approval, the Autodelta safety tank's heavy weight discouraged designers and it was never widely used. A sad fact, since in a parallel demonstration a controlled explosion resulted in the complete destruction of a conventional tank, whereas the Autodelta tank failed to combust at all.

For the 1973 season new regulations came into force requiring a crushable structure to be fitted around the entire fuel tank area. The rules demanded that its structure should be of a sandwich construction with a fire-resistant core and that it should have a minimum crushing strength of 25 lbs per square inch and a minimum thickness of 10 cm. Further rule changes in the mid-Seventies regarding the maximum capacity of a single fuel tank, followed by the introduction of ground effect technology, led to a major change in the design of racing cars for major international categories. Increasingly designers employed a single, centrally-mounted fuel cell, positioned well out of harm's way between the cockpit and the engine. In addition to improving protection of the tank, weight distribution and handling also benefited.

It was only with the reversion to normally aspirated Formula One engines running unlimited fuel, together with a rule requiring the positioning of a driver's feet behind the centre line of the front wheels, that Grand

Prix racing saw the re-introduction of side-mounted fuel tanks. Strictly speaking the new generation tanks were an expansion of the established central tank sideways, in the case of Ferrari a measure made necessary by the excessive length of a V12 engine, and given the desire to maintain a wheelbase length that would not compromise handling. Unfortunately Gerhard Berger's accident during the 1989 San Marino Grand Prix provided a graphic display of the vulnerability of such side-extended fuel tanks.

Berger's Ferrari left the road at high speed on the fourth lap of the race. The impact with the guard rail was taken initially on the right front wheel, which tore off at the suspension pick-up points, as it was designed to do. Alas, the right side-mounted water radiator positioned aft of the wheel was then pushed back along the side of the cockpit, peeling back the part of the fuel tank positioned along that side. This peeling eventually resulted in the rubberised cell tearing high up near the driver's right shoulder. Fuel sprayed out as the tank was almost completely full, and it ignited. Remarkably, given the (heavily televised) ferocity of the fire, only 10 gallons of fuel were calculated to have burned.

As demonstrated by the Berger incident, a cell formed from a rubberised Kevlar bladder is essentially leakproof, crushproof and explosion-proof, but under certain circumstances it can be torn, hence the importance of its container. Formula One regulations require the encasement of the cell in a crushable structure. Similar principles are applied to the other international racing categories and can be usefully applied to all areas of motorsport: the better protected the fuel cell, the less the risk of fire in an accident.

Having established the importance of the cell construction and location, careful consideration to safety in the planning and execution of the rest of the fuel system is of no less significance.

When fitted into the tank, the cell also houses pick-ups, often one at each corner, sometimes pre-pumps and typically one or more filters and a collector pot. The collector, supplied by an inertia feed or the pre-pumps, delivers fuel through non-return valves to the main pump. Other elements of the system are the breather and filler pipes which need to extend to the outside of the car body.

Whenever a fuel feed passes through the cockpit it

In she comes, and in goes the fuel. Pit stop for a Rothmans Porsche 956 Group C car.

should be via steel tubing. The fuel system has to be designed with safety in mind. As Alan Staniforth says, 'visualise a heavy impact ending upside down and feel confident that your work will not allow a drop of fuel to get at you. Work put into this is worth much more than any set of fire-proof overalls'.

The amateur builder may be forced to employ a metal tank. In this case it should be skinned with a generous layer of glassfibre and should be located by beefed-up mounting brackets or extra bracing bars. The use of glassfibre will not prevent the tank becoming punctured but will cut down the flow of fuel. In all race and rally cars the tank must be located out of the cockpit area and there should always be a firewall between tank and driver.

When a car is unlikely to make a pit stop for fuel, a positive-locking or screw-in filler cap is safest. Otherwise the optimum solution is the dry break valve as used in World Championship endurance racing since 1970. Its use was pioneered by the Ferrari team. The Ferrari 512M had sponson tanks either side of the cockpit and for the introduction of dry break valving these were linked by a big bore cross pipe. Each tank was fitted with a female dry break valve. Fuel was fed in on one side through the corresponding bayonet-type male valve, while on the other side an overflow bottle was plugged in via its own male valve. As fuel was fed in, both tanks filled simultaneously, a small bore air pressure balance pipe linking the tops of the tanks. Eventually fuel could be seen spilling into the overflow. Both male valves were then promptly withdrawn, the Avery Hardoll design ensuring that no fuel spilled (hence dry break). Clearly the tanks would now be full to the brim. Since the dry-break and overflow bottle system was introduced on the 512M at Kyalami late in the 1970 season, its use has become universal for endurance racing. Refuelling has also been seen in Formula One along the same lines with planned fuel stops a part of Grand Prix racing in the mid-Eighties.

Endurance racing in the early Seventies also witnessed high pressure refuelling, a technique used in Indy Car racing until it was banned in 1965. Some rigs were capable of blasting a 50 gallon load from storage tank to car in under 10 seconds at 400 p.s.i. The consequence of a hose bursting loose during refuelling need only be imagined to appreciate how hazardous this practice was. Endurance regulations subsequently stated that fuel could only be transferred by a gravity feed with the storage tank no more than 60" above the pit floor. That slowed things down somewhat. Before the height clause, at the 1971 Monza 1000 Kilometres, Gulf Porsche built a tower almost 10 metres high from which to dump its fuel. A 100 litre tank load went down a 100mm. bore pipe in less than 12 seconds. The fuel went in with a wallop, the car lurched down on its springs and the chassis creaked as the g.r.p. bodywork around the tank bowed out.

By way of contrast, Group C regulations for the Eighties set a maximum flow rate of 50 litres per minute, thus it took two long minutes fully to fill the maximum size 100 litre fuel tank. Pit stops in Group C races tended to be a flurry of frantic activity as the car came to a halt, and wheels and drivers were changed and systems were checked, fizzling out into a tense wait for refuelling to finish.

Still the fuel goes in. A maximum rate of refuelling meant that it took two minutes to fill the 100 litre tank.

Gear Shift

The Porsche PDK transmission: many advantages for racing, but a significant weight penalty.

A Grand Prix driver can expect to make something in the region of 2,000 gear changes during a street race such as the Monaco Grand Prix. That averages out around the rate of one every four seconds. Nevertheless, there has been little development in racing gearboxes since the Sixties and there is not much time to be lost or found in established models. These come off the shelf, well-proven and ready to run and everyone starts equal.

Typically, the mid-engine racing car employs a Hewland gearbox which runs without any form of synchromesh. Synchromesh adds weight, creates heat and slows changes. Synchromesh is, however, featured on Porsche racing 'boxes since the company owns a worldwide patent for a system which it licenses and likes to promote as 'used in racing'. Porsche synchromesh gearboxes are extremely reliable and the patent system has many Le Mans wins to its credit, but it has never made inroads into single seater racing.

The harshness of the dog-engagement Hewland 'box bottom gear can make getting underway difficult for a novice. However, a Hewland racing 'box is soon mastered, and it is easily 'rowed' without the clutch. This can cause a certain amount of abuse unless the driver is sensitive enough to modulate the throttle so that engine and road speed are properly matched. A synchromesh gearbox is more heavily abused when used without the clutch and its gear ratios cannot be changed so easily. If a gearbox is of road-car origin it is likely to need a certain amount of beefing up to survive the rigours of racing, and the driver will have to be very sympathetic towards it.

For serious competition, there is little alternative to the Hewland, though Weismann, Staffs and March do produce gearboxes for certain applications. Pete Weismann has long championed the transverse 'box which was first seen in Indy Car racing, later on the Alfa Romeo-Brabham Grand Prix car of the early Eighties. Brabham designer Gordon Murray later incorporated a Weismann transverse gearbox in the Brabham BT55 of 1986 and after he had moved to McLaren International he set his former Brabham assistant David North about the design of a Weismann-based transverse transaxle for the 3.5 litre V10 Honda-McLaren.

The Weismann-derived McLaren gearbox emerged in mid-1989, by which time Hewland and Staffs based bespoke transverse 'boxes were common in Formula One for packaging reasons. The Weismann approach was notable from the driver's point of view for a unique, quick-shift mechanism which did away with the usual spring-loaded plungers, but Weismann and Murray kept details of this innovation a closely-guarded secret.

Fully automatic gearboxes, with the driver selecting 'drive' and leaving the rest to technology, have never been developed for racing. Nor have continuously variable transmission systems (though the DAF infinitely variable belt transmission was toyed with by a Sixties Formula Three racer). Chaparral came closest to the automatic gearbox with its two speed, clutchless transmission, which is described in the Clutch section. The continuously variable transmission may be the thing of the future, though Paul van Valkenburgh has suggested it could cost a fuel consumption penalty, explaining that a surprising amount of fuel is saved in engine 'downtime' during conventional shifting.

The trend of the Eighties has been towards the development of clutchless, push-button gear shifting. Ferrari raced such a system in its 1989 Formula One car, while Porsche had a road and race system known as PDK. PDK stands for Porsche Doppel-Kupplung, or double clutch, and that refers to the fact that two small clutches are employed for gear selection while a conventional clutch is used to disconnect the transmission from the engine. The two selector clutches sit at the front of the box and drive concentric input shafts. The input shafts carry positively-driven gears which constantly mesh with the respective gear on the output shaft. The gears on the output shaft are free to rotate until selected by a dog clutch.

The basic principles of operation are straightforward. If the gearbox is in first gear, the clutch driving second gear will be free. Thus, if the driver wishes to select second, the second gear dog can be safely engaged before the first gear dog is released. Then the second gear selector clutch is progressively taken up while the first gear clutch is progressively freed. Finally, the first gear dog is released. Clearly this system allows gear changing under full load and the conventional clutch is only for starting.

Porsche had to devise fully electronic control to make it work. The selector clutches and dogs are operated by an electronically-governed actuation system and the electronically requested shifts are as good as instant. The necessary hydraulic pump saps a little power but otherwise the system is as efficient as a regular gearbox – if somewhat heavier – but with the same speed, ease and flexibility of changing ratios.

The control system was designed to actuate the twin clutches only at matching engine and road speeds, allowing the driver to pre-select gears via a steering wheel push-button facility. The driver should always find himself in the right gear. If not, he simply punches the appropriate button. Changing gear under load not only dispenses with the need for the clutch but opens up the possibility of changing gear mid-way through a corner without unsettling the car. The electronic control removes the danger of damaging the engine through premature downshifting.

For its PDK-equipped 962C Sports-Prototype Porsche provided two steering wheel push-buttons, one for up shifts, the other for down shifts. A digital display on the dashboard told the driver what gear was engaged and the next gear selected. Flat out in fifth (top), the driver could punch the down button three times for a triple change down to second, the gears not engaging until road speed had fallen appropriately. Gear changing was foolproof and effortless. However, drawbacks of this clutchless, semi-automatic system in racing were increased fuel consumption, a significant weight penalty and, with the complicated electronic control system, there was more to go wrong.

Porsche introduced PDK to its 962C programme in the mid-Eighties and had some success with it after a lightning programme – reducing its penalty to 15 kg – Hans Stuck winning the 1987 German Supercup Group C sprint series. The factory subsequently pulled its works team from Group C racing but PDK development continued for use in fully automatic form in road cars.

Gloves

In an accident involving fire the gloves are usually the first thing to go into the flames as the driver pushes on hot bodywork to lever himself out of the cockpit.

Long Nomex gauntlet-type gloves clearly offer the best fire protection. These should be made from multiple layers of Nomex. As a minimum, three layers is advisable, with leather palms for grip over double layer Nomex. Leather gloves are not fire resistant and the hide will shrink down into direct contact with the skin if worn without lining layers. A generous overlap on to the sleeves of the racing suit is also necessary to prevent riding down and the exposure of the vulnerable wrist area. A drawback, however, of wearing proper fire resistant gloves is that the driver might find himself at a disadvantage while trying to escape in a hurry.

Frank Gardner didn't wear fire resistant gloves for that reason, following a shunt and fire in a racing saloon car. He explains thus: 'To get out of that car I needed everything working for me. I couldn't afford a fumble undoing my belts. Seat belts and door handles had to be operated in split seconds...'

Bob Tullius had a spectacular shunt at Daytona in 1985, driving a Jaguar XJR5. Tyre deflation was to blame and burning pieces of metal and other debris were strewn all over the track. Alight, the wrecked car's bodywork began to deform and, while the cockpit fire extinguisher acted properly, Tullius found he couldn't get the door open. Fearing suffocation, he threw off his helmet to put his head through the side window. Having torn off his gloves to act faster, he suffered burns to his hands, but thankfully only minor ones.

Jackie Stewart was one of the first professional drivers to wear fire resistant gloves. Heavy, thick gloves rather than the thin leather type traditionally favoured by the virtuosi of the steering wheel. Stewart's success put paid to the myth of the need for 'sensitive' gloves. Stewart always wore 'Bury and Hopwood gloves, made by a nice man in the Midlands who is a member of the Worshipful Company of Glove Makers'. Stewart warns against the use of gloves that are not fire resistant, saying: 'Leather

Gloves are primarily for protection in the event of fire. Badly damaged palms cannot be repaired.

gloves in a fire will frizzle up and just melt. The palm of your hand cannot be brought back. The backs of your hands are a little easier. No plastic surgeon today can give you good hands if the palms have been badly burnt. The palm is very difficult to repair.'

Interviewed after his accident at the San Marino Grand Prix in 1989, Gerhard Berger explained that the burns he received to his hands were caused by burning fuel penetrating his gloves. Although of multi-layer construction for the most part, in some areas his gloves were of only a single layer. Fortunately his hands were saved by skilful plastic surgery and a full recovery was made.

Gloves should be multi-layer construction for maximum fire resistance.

Head restraint is vital to avoid whiplash injury.

Head Restraint

Eighties FIA Formula One Regulations required a car to be fitted with a head rest to withstand a rearward force of 85kg. without compression of more than 50mm. A similar precaution will benefit club driver and specail builder. Although deceleration and g-forces may be considerably less in the lower levels of the sport very serious inertia related injuries can be prevented by the provision of adequate head restraint and neck support.

Padded collars fitted below the bottom edge of the crash helmet used only to be worn by a driver suffering an old neck injury. The advent of ground effect and the consequent leap in cornering speed gave rise to neck problems for Formula One and Indy Car competitors. The use of a collar helped to alleviate the forces bearing down on the helmet, which under cornering at ultra high speed can create the effect of placing a large concrete block on the driver's head!

This phenomenon was encountered first by drivers in races on the American high speed oval courses such as Indianapolis. Various methods were tried to combat the tendency of the head to lean inwards when cornering. One method still in use today is to tether the helmet to the sides of the cockpit. This, of course, raises the question of how fast a driver would be able to escape in an emergency. It seems that this is a risk some drivers are willing to take.

Other methods to combat 'g' force include sophisticated designs of combined head rest and neck support and heavily padded areas around the sides of the cockpit near the drivers head.

Helmets

Classic helmet: a hemispherical dome as pioneered by polo players. Leather patches cover the ears.

Back in the early days of motorsport, headgear ranged from non-existant to cloth caps set at a jaunty angle, professionals generally using linen flying caps. A few enlightened drivers tried protective helmets as used by the motorcycling fraternity, but such precautions were generally considered unnecessary for car racing. Indeed, crash helmets did not become mandatory until the early Fifties, following a series of accidents causing head injuries to the victims.

Since that time the crash helmet has evolved from a crude, hemispherical dome perched on the top of the head to a sophisticated piece of hi-tech equipment. These days it is tailor-made from space-age materials, is capable of protecting the head from heavy impact and, if so equipped, is able to provide a breathable atmosphere in a fire.

Early helmets were adaptations of protective headgear used in other sports, particularly polo. Those used by Moss, Fangio and their contemporaries consisted of a cork lined dome, with an integral peak. Sometimes shellac coated layers of cotton and wool felt were employed. This hemispherical design offered protection for the top of the head, above the eyes and ears. The latter were covered by leather flaps which formed part of the strap and harness which held the helmet in place.

The early Sixties saw this design superseded by the 'pilot' type as exemplified by the Bell helmet worn by Fangio and Moss' successor, Jim Clark, at this time. The protective shell was made of laminated glass fibre cloth with a plastic resin coating and had a lining of expanded polystyrene foam. This design offered rigid protection over the ears and temples. Press-studs fitted to the helmet allowed a range of peaks and visors to be fitted to a driver's personal requirements.

At Indianapolis in May 1968, Dan Gurney was one of the first to wear a Bell Star, the original full face 'integral'-type helmet. At the wet German Grand Prix later in the year, Gurney introduced the Bell Star to Formula One. In the conservative Old World he caused a sensation, looking like an alien from a space movie. However, within a year most of the top Grand Prix drivers were wearing a full face-type helmet and by the end of the 1971 season, open face helmets were a rare sight in most international racing categories.

Since the inception of the full-face helmet, the basic design has remained essentially unchanged. Further refinements have occurred such as adaption for life support systems (qv) and radio systems, while there have been a wide variety of sizes and shapes of eye slit. A smaller slit in theory offers better protection in the event of a fire but it is more claustrophobic. Typically, manufacturers offer a range of slit depths and widths.

In the mid-Seventies, Griffin marketed a helmet with such a large opening that it was virtually an open face helmet with a protective bar across the chin. At the other extreme, in the late Seventies Bell produced a full-face helmet with a narrow eye slot divided by a bar (concealing the bridge of the nose) and claimed to offer protection against flying catch fencing poles.

Perhaps the most famous, certainly the most eye-catching design seen to date, is the Simpson RX1, or 'Star Wars' helmet as it became popularly known. This featured a unique integral face mask which incorporated special filters to protect the driver from the danger of inhaling flames and heat. Originally it also featured a built-in Nomex bib but this was discarded from later designs as it proved difficult to keep clean with regular use.

More recently, with the wider use of advanced materials such as carbon fibre and Kevlar, much development work by manufacturers has gone into reducing the overall weight of helmets. The era of high downforce racing cars highlighted the weight problem, enormous g-forces causing great discomfort and neck problems for drivers. These were brought about by the crash helmet assuming the weight of a large concrete block when cornering at levels of g-force previously unencountered.

Ventilation can be a problem for the wearer of a full-face helmet. Manufacturers have tried to solve the problem in various ways but the effectiveness of any solution must be doubtful in single-seater use, given that the cockpit cowling is invariably designed to throw air over the driver's head to prevent buffeting. Also, it can be argued that perforations as widely incorporated for ventilation should be kept to a minimum to avoid

The first space age
Grand Prix driver.
Dan Gurney
pioneered the fully
enveloping helmet
in Formula One.

weakening the helmet. Open face helmets obviously provide better ventilation but seriously reduce protection.

A number of competitors use open-face helmets in touring car and Sports-Prototype racing, but the improved ventilation must be measured against the possible consequences of an accident involving a heavy impact or fire. Despite harness restraint a driver's face can make contact with the steering wheel or gear lever, while the cockpit will likely be showered with glass fragments from the windscreen. A fire in an enclosed cockpit produces heat and fumes against which an open face helmet and balaclava would offer little protection.

An easily and quickly operated flame resistant strap is the usual method of holding the helmet on the head. French manufacturer GPA produced a helmet with a hinged flap front and rear, which not only fixed it on the head but also provided a good seal against fire. However, the ease of removing such a helmet in an emergency is open to question: with the conventional method the strap can be easily cut.

All helmets used in competition are required to conform to BSI Standard 2495 or equivalent, such as the French AFNOR, German ONS or the American Snell Foundation SA (Special Application) standards. All of these bodies arrange for stringent tests for impact resistance, penetration resistance, fire resistance and chin strap strength.

A typical modern helmet has an outer shell of either laminated fibreglass or, in some instances, layers of carbon fibre and Kevlar over a non-resilient liner of expanded polystyrene foam. On impact the foam is designed to collapse at a progressive rate, protecting the wearer from injury by preventing the transmission of shock loading to the brain. Surprisingly, a soft, padded liner of foam rubber would actually be more harmful as it could cause injury by rebounding the driver's head inside the helmet.

As the liner is non-resilient, any helmet involved in an impact – even if only accidentally dropped – should not be used again until checked and cleared by the manufacturer. A flame-resistant material covers the polystyrene liner and adds comfort for the wearer.

A flame resistant balaclava worn beneath the helmet is another vital piece of equipment. FIA regulations require a minimum of two layers of material and that the balaclava be tested to ISO 6940. A range of shapes and sizes of eye holes are available. A fire-proof bib attached to the bottom of the helmet by Nomex velcro is a worthwhile extra layer of protection. If the helmet is equipped with a life support system a bib is vital to provide a seal to exclude heat and fumes (see Life Support).

For a helmet to do its job correctly it must fit correctly. It is not advisable to buy a helmet by mail order since measurements vary from manufacturer to manufacturer and even from helmet to helmet. While a comfortable fit is essential, it must not be so comfortable that the helmet moves around on the head. It should also be remembered that on a hot day the head may swell slightly.

A helmet has a useful life of between one and six years. Some helmets are prone to deterioration through exposure to ultra violet light, some through extremes of temperature and some chemically decompose. Any helmet used in the UK in an RAC MSA-administered event must carry a sticker showing an expiry date after which the helmet can no longer be used. The RAC MSA scheme allows a maximum of four years. While a newly-purchased helmet is given a four-year sticker, older helmets presented to scrutineers must have their age proven, so that the appropriate shorter life sticker can be applied.

Helmet painting and the application of decals should be carried out with great care as the chemical composition of paints and adhesives can weaken the outer shell. Painting should only be carried out by a reputable helmet decorating specialist. A modern helmet is a necessarily expensive item and should be carefully looked after. Storage in a rigid container when not in use is advisable, while a proper helmet bag to carry it around will prevent scratching or minor damage.

*Instrumentation
should be simple yet
effective, like this.
The computer
based Stack rev
counter has
traditional analogue
read out.*

Instrumentation

Instruments and warning lights exist to provide the driver with vital information. Too much information can distract from the job in hand – racing – so the more concise the message, the better for the driver. Ideally he should be given no more than is essential – r.p.m., oil pressure and water temperature – via gauges, everything else can be monitored via warning lights with a back-up light for oil pressure. Oil pressure and water temperature can be combined in a simple, effective arrangement that can be positioned centrally. Oil temperature and fuel pressure might be added but a tachometer plus four gauges is starting to overload the driver's attention. Rarely does he need to know oil temperature under normal racing conditions. As David Kennedy says, 'A lot of information is OK while stationary in the pits but when racing I tend to ignore much of it.'

Fuel pressure gauges have been known to suffer ruptured diaphragms when monitoring high pressure injection systems such as the Bosch Kugel-fischer mechanical and electro-mechanical systems which work at 40 bar. Gauges must be reliable, accurate and easy to read. Each gauge must be clearly labelled and the danger zone needs to be marked in red. The normal operating condition should register as a vertical needle.

Proper calibration of all gauges is essential and the rev counter must be checked to ensure there is less than 1% error at top revs. Inexpensive rev counters are dubious at the top end; cable-driven or electronics are essential. Instrument panels must be insulated against vibration. Night competitors will need effective instrument lighting with a dimmer switch facility.

A typical example of a contemporary instrumentation system is that fitted to the TWR Jaguar XJR V12 prototype. TWR employed Smiths instruments, the tachometer, flanked by oil and water gauges, visible through the steering wheel, together with warning lights to indicate low oil pressure and low fuel pressure. Oil and fuel pressure gauges and a volt meter were positioned ahead of the passenger seat. A gearbox temperature gauge was tried early on but was found to be an unnecessary distraction given little temperature fluctuation, and it was soon replaced by a simple warning light.

In 1986 the XJR6 became one of the first cars to run the so-called 'intelligent tachometer' developed by Stack Ltd of Bicester, England, and Maryland, USA. The Stack rev counter looked conventional enough, but had an in-built micro-processor which used quartz timing to measure engine speed and, in addition to running a unique 'no waver' needle drive, monitored engine revs and recorded the data for subsequent display via a portable computer and printer. The system called for the driver to create reference points on a lap by pushing a button. At the end of the run, the information was printed out in graph form.

TWR developed a tyre pressure monitor in conjunction with its engine management specialist Zytek and this is described in the wheel and tyre section.

The development of engine management systems led to digital instrumentation replacing conventional gauges with a sophisticated digital system; a single read-out ahead of the driver could provide a range of information as requested, together with a constant r.p.m. monitor. The Pi digital display developed by Pi in the Eighties in conjunction with Lola Cars was one such system.

In addition to its use in the Lola-built Nissan GC89, the Pi system was used by a number of other Sports-Prototype teams, including Mazdaspeed. Mazdaspeed chassis designer Nigel Stroud incorporated it in his design for its ability to monitor 'every aspect of chassis management from ride height to tyre temperatures'. Usually operating in tachometer mode, the display could be switched to show information requested by the driver at the touch of a button. Additionally, reaching a pre-set threshold on any of the systems being monitored automatically triggered a warning light. At the sight of the light the appropriate display was selected by the driver. Depending on the encroachment, the threshold could be re-set higher, but if the light was triggered again it would imply that it would be wise to visit the pits at the soonest opportunity. Mazdaspeed driver David Kennedy says in praise, 'the Pi computer system is a way of filtering information. In the past there were so many dials that it was not always possible to assimilate everything and take action.'

On the Nissan the Pi display was augmented by

analogue engine temperature gauges while, conversely, the contemporary Aston Martin Group C car used a traditional dial rev counter with a pair of custom-made LCD units for other readings, with the fuel read-out programmed to over-ride when a critical threshold was crossed.

The question as to whether the modern racing car needs highly sophisticated instrumentation was posed at Le Mans in 1989 when Aston Martin driver David Leslie drove his car for five laps early in the race with the dashboard completely removed after it was damaged by an electrical fire. Waiting for dashboard repairs Leslie was lapping at close to normal speeds reliant on his senses to keep the engine within its rev limit. A balancing view, however, comes from rival Mazdaspeed driver David Kennedy, who disclosed that during the first hour of the same race his Pi system over-ride flashed up a right rear tyre temperature far in excess of normal. Despite reducing speed to 100 m.p.h. instead of the more normal 200 m.p.h., the car still went sideways negotiating the Mulsanne Kink...

In Formula One, as in Group C, the principle is one of providing minimum interference of a driver's concentration. In 1989 March used the Stack system, as did many other teams, March running it in conjunction with a secondary LCD unit displaying temperatures and pressures. Meanwhile, McLaren used a bespoke tachometer which took the form of a series of lights in an arc, with a digital display below for fluid temperatures and pressures.

Intercom

The use of intercoms was pioneered in rallying for communication between driver and co-driver. Systems were relatively inexpensive and lightweight, yet rugged enough to stand up to the inevitable abuse. Intercoms began to appear in the pit lane at Grands Prix in the mid-Seventies, McLaren in particular having had experience of their use in Indy car racing. These days the pit lane intercom is used throughout professional racing and any aspiring team would do well to acquire one, given relatively low cost and obvious benefits. In a noisy pit lane a multiway conversation between driver, team manager and any other relevant personnel plugged into the system is possible, without any party needing to raise their voice. In the past team members required the lung power and projection of Pavarotti to make themselves understood at times.

The intercom system on the driver's side usually consists of earphones mounted in the padded earpieces of the helmet, this arrangement allowing the driver to wear conventional ear plugs. Some favour earphones inserted directly into the ear in the manner of some personal stereos. The microphone, of the noise cancelling type, is mounted on the forward bar section of the helmet which protects the driver's lower facial area. In the case of an open face helmet – used by some sports prototype and touring car drivers – the microphone is mounted on a stalk projecting from the side of the helmet. Throat microphones have also been used, with inconclusive results.

In the pits the team manager and other personnel connected to the system have lightweight headphones and microphones with noise protection earphones. Once connected by a regular jack plug connection, the driver pushes a conveniently-situated button, typically on a steering wheel spoke to complete the link-up, and the words of wisdom can flow.

Damon Hill gets plugged in. His famous father didn't have such equipment during his early days.

*A rare sight in late
Eighties Grand Prix
racing: a driver
using a life support
system. This is
Mansell, of course*

Life Support System

When it emerged that Jo Siffert had died from asphyxiation in his burning BRM that fateful day at Brands Hatch in 1971, it became a priority to devise a way of allowing the driver breathing time. Time to escape from or be rescued from a burning car, or at least for the flames to be quenched. To do this it was clearly necessary to supply useable air. This could be done inside a fully enveloping helmet: the aim was to supply a breathable atmosphere, at the same time repelling the encroachment of toxic fumes and heat.

Graviner, the fire extinguisher manufacturer, won a major Motor Sport Safety Award for its pioneering life support system which supplied sixty seconds of air to a driver's crash helmet in the event of fire. Graviner's innovation recognised that an on-board fire extinguisher system can only do so much. Cars are liable to become engulfed in flames that need fire marshals with more substantial equipment to combat.

A driver's flame retardant clothing should give him at least a minute's protection from a fire but as the seconds tick by death through asphyxiation is an increasing real danger. Fire eats oxygen. Even if injuries and burns are minor, the lack of oxygen can cause permanent damage. Death can also be caused by inhalation of flames, smoke and toxic fumes. Hence the need for medical air which does not burn. The so-called life support system essentially consists of an air bottle, a release valve and a flame resistant tube running into a helmet fitting. The aim is to supply medical air to the driver, even if he should be unconscious.

The positive pressure inside the helmet keeps out heat and fumes. However, for the system to operate effectively it must be used in conjunction with a flame resistant bib attached to the bottom of the helmet so as to create a seal around the driver's neck.

Soon after the Graviner breakthrough, Intercontinental Safety Equipment, manufacturers of Fireater extinguishers and Sabre industrial breathing apparatus, introduced its own system, claimed to be lighter and to pump air at twice the rate for the same sixty second period.

Life support systems have become obligatory in most if not all International Formulae but their use is not universal and some drivers have expressed doubts over their safety. Some have cited the risk of the air supply feeding a fire, turning the helmet – and head – into a ball of flame. If the supply were pure oxygen this might be the case, but as compressed medical air is used to avoid this danger the argument would appear fallacious. Others have claimed that the connection of the feed tube to their helmet would impede their exit in an emergency – yet happily connect themselves by a cable to their car's on-board radio!

Current Formula One regulations typically make the fitting of an air bottle obligatory but its use is optional, although recommended by the FIA Safety Commission. In spite of Gerhard Berger's graphic demonstration of the worth of a life support system at Imola in 1989, the only drivers to use them on a regular basis at following races that season appeared to be Berger and his team-mate Nigel Mansell. Our investigations revealed that many drivers still subscribe to the arguments cited above.

McLaren drivers had not used life support systems for many years. Niki Lauda, it was surprisingly revealed, had been vehemently against using such apparatus during his days with the team. As evidenced by Berger's accident, a fire in an open cockpit car is perhaps more survivable than in an enclosed Prototype or suchliké. A fire in a coupé would burn out all the oxygen in a short time. However, when canvassed on the subject during the 1989 season, few Group C Sports-Prototype drivers were found to be using life support. As in Formula One, fitting the system was mandatory but its use was not.

Mario Andretti
plugged in. The
American star has
always been
conscious of safety.

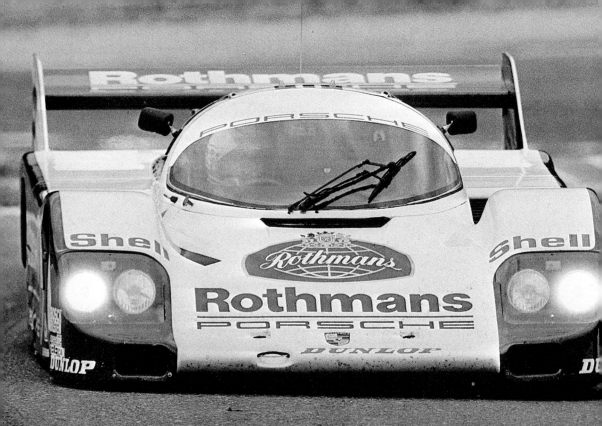

Lights

Night racing is rare these days but good lighting is one of the primary considerations of any rally competitor. Headlights must be quartz halogen rather than tungsten for maximum brightness and should be 100 watt for power, though a high rating tends to mean a shorter life. Clearly headlights should be set up with the car fully laden. Le Mans runners have been known to find high-speed nose droop upsetting headlight settings.

Rally competitors must consider other road users when designing and using uprated lighting systems. A system with auxiliary lamps may require a more powerful alternator. This must be carefully installed with the correct bracket, bolts and pulley and with the control box and regulator checked and adjusted to suit the power and the battery, since over-charging is as bad as under-charging.

The auxiliary lights must be firmly mounted and there should be relays built into the circuit to cope with the loading. These reduce the voltage drop and take the load off the switches. Check that the wire is up to the job, too. Lamp fuses are not essential and certainly not all lamps should be on the same fuse to avoid sudden darkness! Fog and spotlights should be wired to go out on dip beam.

These days even single seaters require red rear lights and these should be rubber mounted, along with everything else prone to vibration failure.

At Le Mans Mazda uses Cibie head lamps in custom-built pods. The lights are adjustable in that they can be reset while the car is stationary in the pits, though there is no provision made for adjustment while the car is in motion. The internals of the indicators and brake lights come from a Mazda road car and are fitted inside specially-made plastic lenses.

Nissan mounted its rear lights atop the rearmost edge of the venturi tunnels on its '89 Group C Prototype, thus alleviating the necessity of disconnecting them each time the engine cover was removed.

Lights are not only for the night: Sports-Prototype aces use them to clear a path...

Mirrors

Sensible sized mirrors: setting them high affords good rearward vision. But at what aerodynamic cost?

The regulations concerning rear view mirrors in Grand Prix racing have traditionally been vague. Today a minimum mirror surface area is specified for Formula Three, Formula 3000 and Group C Prototypes yet the designer of a Formula One car is able to fulfill the requirements of the regulations by providing two mirrors of any size giving rearward vision. In some cases these mirrors are of such miniscule dimensions as to call their effectiveness into question.

With the rise to pre-eminence of aerodynamics in the Seventies, mirror sizes began to be reduced. The loss of a few square millimetres of frontal area was found to be significant enough to improve aerodynamic efficiency usefully through drag reduction. Previously rearward vision had been catered for by the fitting of sensibly sized mirrors, the emphasis on providing a view rather than airflow. The 1971 championship-winning Tyrrell of Jackie Stewart had mirrors mounted high above the cockpit on pylons, offering rearward vision on either side of the rear aerofoil.

The modern Grand Prix car features mirrors mounted in the more traditional location on either side of the cockpit coaming with the rear view taken from below the rear wing. In the case of a number of 1989 designs the mirrors were certainly so small as to afford negligible view. In the case of Ligier this must have served to make a bad situation worse on a few occasions: one of its drivers was already acknowledged as very difficult to pass and he can hardly have been aided by mirrors barely the size of matchboxes!

In Group C prototype racing, a minimum of 100mm^2 mirror area is required by the regulations, prompting one designer to describe the mirrors used on his own '89 design as 'barn doors'. Some teams have experimented with electronically adjustable mirrors for endurance events. Nissan discarded this option after initial tests, considering it yet another electrical system liable to failure. Jaguar and Aston Martin have raced with such a system, finding it particularly advantageous when running driver pairings of different heights.

In the late Sixties, the Len Bailey-designed Ford F3L prototype had a single mirror mounted on its roof and viewed through a transparent panel in the cockpit ceiling, a configuration also used by Ferrari on its 512 Sports coupé.

For the amateur builder aerodynamic considerations will probably be less important. Sensibly-sized and positioned mirrors are essential, particularly on mixed test days.

*Mirrors, late Eighties
Formula One style.
Matchbox sized and
of dubious
effectiveness.*

Pit Signals

When the Gordon Murray designed Brabham BT46 was unveiled at the end of 1977, in addition to its revolutionary surface cooling system, it also featured a dashboard LCD unit on which lap times and other information could be passed to the driver. This innovation caused predictions in some quarters of the end of the use of the traditional pit signalling board. The idea did not get beyond the prototype stage. Over a decade later the pit board is still in universal use throughout motor racing. A somewhat surprising fact, given the pace of technological innovation, particularly in Grand Prix racing. The pit signalling board was first seen in use in the Thirties when the Mercedes and Auto Union teams established new standards in team strategy and organisation.

The key information shown on the board is usually a car's current position in the race and time intervals to the cars immediately ahead and behind, the former expressed as a negative value, the latter as a positive. Additionally, the number of laps remaining in the race, or in an endurance event the number of laps remaining until the next scheduled pit stop, are important. Of course, the time for the previous lap completed may be shown during the race as well as in practice. The board is also useful for conveying reminders to the driver, who in the heat of battle may have forgotten, for example, to switch off an electric fuel pump. Given that the driver generally will be passing the signalling area at high speed, the data must be displayed in as clear and easily-read form as possible. The board should carry some means to enable it to be picked out from a multitude of others as the driver flashes by.

As to why teams continue to rely on this throwback to the heroic age of motor sport, opinion is divided. Obviously not all teams, particularly those in the lesser formulae, could afford the electronics necessary to supersede the pit board. It is, after all, an efficient and reliable way of passing information. However, the answer may be simpler still; as one driver put it, 'When you see the board each lap, at least you know someone is watching what you're doing, even if you're five laps behind the leader.'

In spite of the widespread use of pits to car radios these days, signal remains an indispensible means of communication.

The race suit is for protection and for selling. For these drivers, at a very high price...

Race Suits

In an accident involving burning fuel a driver can be subjected to temperatures of up to 2,500 degrees Farenheit. In such circumstances, even wearing flame resistant clothing the best that he can hope for is a minute of protection in which to make his escape.

Until the mid-Sixties genuinely flame resistant overalls were simply not available. In the earliest days of motorsport, overalls were literally that, a garment to keep the clothes worn underneath clean. By the Fifties some of these overalls were being marketed as having 'flame-proof' properties, yet by modern standards they were woefully inadequate.

The search for truly flame resistant materials became a priority in the Sixties after a number of horrific accidents involving fires. The sight of Lorenzo Bandini's blazing Ferrari at the 1967 Monaco Grand Prix (seen on television screens across the world) played no small part in this. Brand names such as Proban, Protex and Nomex became buzz words in motor racing circles. Proban was a cotton fabric treated with tetrakis hydroxymethyl phosphonium chloride, the process giving a useful degree of flame resistance, if weakening the fabric slightly. A similar process applied to a PVC/Nylon mix was called Protex. Nomex was developed by industry in conjunction with the US Naval Air Development Centre as a material primarily to provide thermal protection in flying suits. Known in its prototype form as HT 1, the modified nylon material was produced and marketed by DuPont.

In initial experiments with HT 1-DuPont Nomex, it was found that a single layer offered no better protection than other materials tested. However, on closer inspection it was determined that where there was a double layer of material, such as in seams and pockets, there was an absence of severe heat penetration, resulting in a lesser degree of burning on the test dummy. A complete double-layered suit was found to provide much greater protection than its counterpart. Thus was the most important principle in the use of flame resistant garments established: the necessity to wear multiple layers, partly

because air trapped between the layers acts as insulation.

The minimum is one outer layer to shield against flames, with an inner layer to provide insulation from the heat, the outer layer being of sufficient resistance to prevent the penetration of flames. For Nomex, DuPont claimed that the outer layer when charred formed a carbon crust which protected the layer below from flame and heat.

Exhaustive tests of flame resistant materials were carried out in the early Seventies by the Jim Clark Foundation working with the Hosiery and Allied Trades Association. Their aim was to test the flame resistance of the large number of materials available at the time. Their tests included one to determine the time elapsed before an internal temperature rise of 25°C. Their published findings became the basis of standards for protective clothing in motor sport.

At the time of writing, all race suits used at meetings run to FIA regulations must have passed the tests specified under the *FIA Safety Commission, FIA 1986 standards for heat and flame resistant clothing for competition drivers*, an up-date of previous FIA standards of 1975 and 1980.

These regulations were drafted in 1986 but only became mandatory at the start of the 1988 season. They required the submission by manufacturers of fabric specimens from a given suit, to an FIA-recognised test house. The specimens had to be certified to have been tested to the ISO6940 Standard which measured the ignition and burning of textile fabrics. At the test house the specimens were subjected to tests measuring heat transfer, mechanical resistance and the security of the seams.

The performance requirement for the heat transfer test was the resistance or suppression of heat build-up for 12 or more seconds before a temperature rise sufficient to cause a second degree burn. The mechanical resistance test required the specimen, after exposure to heat, to withstand being bent through 180° at the same spot five times. The seam test measured flame resistance of the thread used in the seams, any melting or flaming resulting in rejection of the whole garment. The same tests were repeated on separate samples of the same fabric which had been laundered 15 times, and on further samples that had been dry-cleaned 15 times.

On successfully passing the tests, the manufacturer

Martin Donnely models the typical Eighties race suit, a multi-layer production in Nomex.

supplied FISA with its certification to that effect and was issued with a homologation number unique to that particular model of race suit. All production examples of the suit had to carry this number in an easily visible position on the upper frontal areas. FISA publishes lists of homologated suits and their performance figures.

Suits are available from various manufacturers in configurations ranging from a single layer up to six layers, sometimes more. However, the greater the number of layers the more cumbersome and restrictive a suit is likely to be.

Most professional drivers favour three- or four-layer suits. In extreme applications such as Top Fuel drag racing, six-layer suits incorporating reflective asbestos, leather, Nomex and a cool suit have been used. DuPont has continued the development of its Nomex material and in 1989 produced 'Nomex 3' which contained 5% Kelvar, for which the manufacturer claimed resistance to tearing even when alight. The addition of Kevlar also made Nomex 3 lighter than its forerunners.

A typical example of a modern-day racing suit is the ST2000 model, made by Stand 21 of Dijon Talant, France, and used by many of the world's top drivers, including World Champions Alain Prost and Ayrton Senna, Indianapolis 500 winner Emerson Fittipaldi and all the crew of the 1989 Le Mans winning Sauber Mercedes.

The style of the suit is similar to that of its rivals. In its construction the ST2000 is unique in that it is made of a special stretched Nomex developed by DuPont exclusively for Stand 21. This material is claimed to be '20–25% more fire resistant for a similar weight' while providing extra ventilation. The outer layer is of knitted Nomex, the intermediate layer of Nomex honeycomb and the internal layer of Jersey Nomex of similar texture to Nomex underwear. The layers are linked by widely-spaced pinstriping.

The practice of pinstriping, and also that of box quilting, although giving a smart appearance, can compromise the effectiveness of a race suit if not done properly. An excess of stitching flattens and compacts the material, making it effectively a single layer. The more air trapped between the layers and in the fibres, the better the insulation.

For a similar reason the addition of sponsors' badges should be carried out with care. Heat bonding is illegal under FIA rules, which recommend that a flame resistant backing be set under each badge. Flame resistant thread should be used to sew badges on. To be carefully avoided is heavy embroidery through the suit, since this will compact the fabrics in the embroidered area.

Nomex velcro is used by manufacturers for wrist, neck and ankle closures. Brass zips are also used as they boast low heat transference. Zips must be mounted on heat resistant backing.

The best suits are tailored to the individual driver and stretch pads are often built in around the shoulders and armpits for ease of movement. Sewn-in shoulder grab handles can help rescuers pull a driver from his car without adding to his injuries. Similar handles can be sewn to the sides and legs of the suit.

A race suit is often a compromise since it has to be practical. It must be reasonably light and comfortable, allow adequate movement, and it must not over-heat the driver in hot conditions. Typically a professional road racing driver will wear a flame retardant three- or four-layer suit, together with flame retardant underwear, both reaching from ankles to neck to wrist. In addition a flame resistant balaclava under the helmet, flame retardant long socks and flame retardant gloves and boots are worn.

For the club driver the same basic principles apply. Multi-layer protection is essential and suits made with plastic zips and non-flame-proof threads must be avoided, as in a fire these would melt and the suit would literally fall apart.

In general, having the race suit and flame retardant underwear loose-fitting aids comfort, as well as improving insulation. This is far more important than having the suit tight fitting in the name of fashion, sponsors or no. For long-distance racing a change of overalls is a good idea and a smothering of talcum powder on the underwear can help avoid sores and chafing.

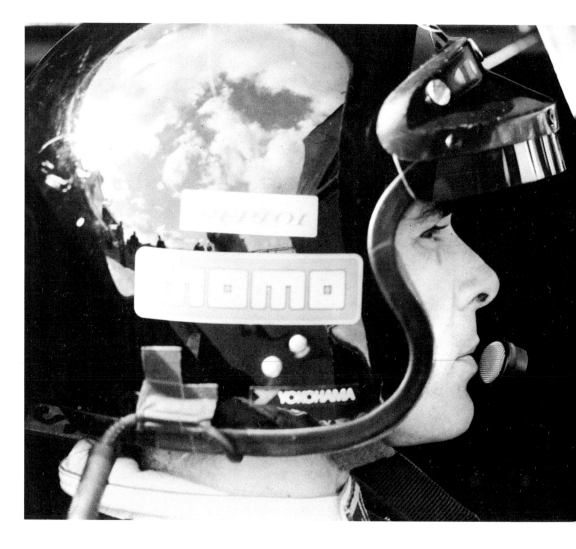

Broadcasting from
the cockpit of a
240m.p.h. projectile
radio communica-
tion is common in
Sports-Prototype
racing

Radios

Team to car radio contact is the obvious extension of pit signals and intercom communication and was exploited first in international rallying, once teams started chasing their runners with service 'barges' and helicopters. The use of short-wave radio for communication between pit and car on a closed circuit is seemingly less crucial given the fact that the car will pass the teams' signalling point once each lap. And rarely do lap times exceed three minutes. However, there is a limit to the amount of information that can be carried on the pit board, and conditions can change within a lap that cause tactics to be re-evaluated. This is particularly true in Indy Car racing with its frequent yellow light periods. Pitting for fuel under a yellow can save time but gains depend upon a car's overall fuel situation and the exact timing and duration of the caution period. Radio contact between team manager and driver is essential if a car is to make the most of caution periods.

Pits to car radio contact only became common in Grand Prix racing following the fuel limitations imposed during the turbo era. Suddenly the driver had to run his race with an eye on the fuel gauge and improved communication with the team manager, while not essential, was a major bonus.

Radio contact means that a driver can warn the pits of the onset of a problem which can cut down the length of the subsequent stop. And it can allow the driver to discuss the wisdom of a wing setting change or other such alteration with his engineer during the course of an endurance event, prior to stopping at the pit. Under general racing conditions the radio is only used by the driver to report problems and discuss tactics but similar use can be made of the system during practice to maximise track time. Another practice use is the transmission of lap times, although this will only be a back-up to the traditional pit signalling board.

When using radio, the driver's helmet, containing headphones and microphone (see Intercom) is connected to a mobile transceiver carefully located on the car to avoid interference between its operation and that of the

The vital links. The steering wheel push button must be plumbed in while the car must carry an aerial.

car's other electrical systems. In the pits the team manager, engineer and other designated personnel are either plugged into the main pits transceiver or carry their own mobiles. The pits transceiver unit is generally a portable battery powered model that can fit inside a strong aluminium briefcase complete with its antenna. The antenna is either set up atop the briefcase or on a better site, such as the roof of the pits via an extension cable. Of course, the effectiveness of short-wave radio depends somewhat upon the terrain, and flat circuits such as Le Mans and Silverstone are ideal.

The sound quality seems to vary considerably. Mazda-speed driver David Kennedy reported favourably on the rig used in the raucous quad-rotor Group C car even when wearing earplugs. On the other hand, in the high-revving Ferrari 640 V12 Formula One car, Nigel Mansell claimed he was unable to hear his team manager telling him to come into the pits during the infamous black flag incident at the 1989 Portuguese Grand Prix.

Driver reaction to the concept is also varied. Australian Touring Car drivers like Dick Johnson and Peter Brock are seemingly happy to chat to millions of TV viewers as they race around the daunting Bathurst circuit. On the other hand, TWR Jaguar driver Armin Hahne at Le Mans in 1986 professed to be too busy to talk even to his team manager as he approached Mulsanne Corner on a quick qualifying lap. Roberto Ravaglia, the 1988 Touring Car Champion, had a novel use for the radio system in his BMW M3; when leading races, he serenaded his team manager with Italian operatic arias!

It is unavoidable that other teams listen to radio communications. An open secret in NASCAR and Indy Car racing, eavesdropping was not readily admitted to at the time of writing by Formula One and Group C teams. In America even the race fans participate; the equipment is available for only a few hundred dollars and the teams are willing to reveal which frequencies they are using.

Short-wave radios have also been used to transmit information from a car's engine management system back to the pits. This is covered in detail in the Telemetry section.

This little device is
the mandatory
F3000 rev limiter
which enforces the
9000r.p.m. limit.

Rev Limiter

A rev limiter is a device to protect the engine rather than assist the driver. It protects the engine by introducing an electrical misfire or cutting the fuel once a certain r.p.m. threshold is reached. In general, the driver should not reach that threshold if he is doing his job properly. However, sometimes power keeps building beyond the safe limit of an engine and it then becomes almost inevitable that the driver will lean on the limiter in the heat of battle.

Rev limiters can be bought off the shelf from companies specialising in engine electronics. These work in conjunction with the ignition, introducing a tiny misfire at a pre-set r.p.m. Where an engine management system is employed, a limiter is invariably in-built. There are various forms it can take. For example, at Le Mans in 1989 the winning Mercedes-Sauber ran a Motronic MP2.7 engine management system which allowed its 5.0 litre turbocharged V8 to climb unhindered to 7,000 r.p.m. Beyond that level the ignition was first retarded, something the driver could sense, and if he ignored that warning the fuel was cut at 7,200 r.p.m. Cutting the fuel was instantaneous since solenoid injectors were employed.

By way of contrast, the rival Joest Porsche team cut the fuel, then the ignition. The Joest car was similarly equipped with fully electronic injection and ran a Motronic MP1.7 system. Its flat six engine (built in-house by Mike Demont) lost its fuel at 8,200 r.p.m., its entire ignition at 8,400 r.p.m. However, a lamp in the cockpit warned the driver well before his engine was shut down!

Roll Cage

The roll cage is a piece of safety equipment that can actually make a car go faster. Even an off-the-shelf roll cage can do much more than merely stop the windscreen pillars collapsing should the car overturn. It can add rigidity to the entire chassis structure, and will add a considerable amount to any production chassis if properly designed and integrated. That rigidity helps further protect the occupants in the event of any accident and gives the chassis usefully enhanced stiffness in torsion and bending. Such stiffness is an important factor in chassis performance. For example, it only requires a fractional relative movement of front and rear suspension pick-up points to make a mockery of theoretical suspension performance.

A production car modified for competition can gain a great deal through exploitation of roll bar technology. Generally, the rules require the roll cage to be in the form of a box but triangulating this for stiffness and connecting it to the front and rear suspension mounts means that a production car can, at the extreme, acquire practically a multi-tubular frame chassis. If body panels can be legally lightened the result is almost a pure competition machine.

Trans Am regulations for the Eighties allowed a tube frame fitted with standard shape metal panels to replace the production shell. While far removed from showroom stock racing, that made for safer cars. Further, allowing such scope for modification assisted the resourceful specialist builder and tended to make the racing more competitive by restricting the scope for one manufacturer to mop up with a vastly expensive homologation special exercise.

The potential of an extensive roll cage inserted within a production shell is well illustrated by the example of the Porsche 935 Group 5 car of the Seventies. This had its 911 production shell well braced by a carefully designed roll cage and it came out with a torsional rigidity better than that previously recorded for the marque's earlier spaceframe 917 Sports-Prototype, a no compromise racer.

Even in the case of the club rally car, an off-the-shelf

The interior of a Group A Ford Sierra Cosworth reveals the regulation roll cage, adding chassis stiffness.

roll cage from a specialist should be bolted into the shell very thoughtfully so as to absorb and spread loads from stress points in it. This will make the car much stiffer and it will be inherently more reliable and longer lived. The weight penalty is rarely a problem, given minimum weight limits, and in any case some form of cage is likely to be mandatory.

It is clear that the cage should not be hurriedly installed with its feet conveniently bolted to the floorpan. The floorpan is invariably a thin metal sheet: the feet should be bolted somewhere more solid or at least to a welded-in plate which turns at right angles somewhere to a different panel. Elsewhere, the tubes should be welded or bolted to the shell to advantage. For example, welded-in nuts can be attached to the screen pillars, matching brackets on the cage to enable it to be bolted firmly to the pillars. Further, the rear suspension can be braced via rear bracing legs of the cage. Overall, the result should be firmer, more precise handling as well as a more rugged car.

On a race track that handling advantage is invaluable. It is worth remembering that, where there are a few specific highly-loaded points to be connected, such as engine mounts and suspension brackets, the spaceframe approach is actually a more efficient solution than moncoque construction. Spaceframes should by no means be considered antiquated technology and any chance to incorporate spaceframe-type strength into a production-based shell must be welcomed.

Steel tubing is generally called for, otherwise where funds are extensive lightweight titanium might be considered. The important point is to use a strong enough material – mild steel tubing will probably suffice – and to stress it properly. A scale model cage in balsa wood can help test alternative solutions. As much triangulation as possible should pay dividends. Where the production shell has to stay intact, it should be seam-welded, while the engine and transmission should be mounted rigidly. It all adds stiffness.

A basic principle of structural engineering tells us that the taller and wider a given structure, the stiffer it will be and thus a bulky production shape lends itself to a stiff tubeframe insert. This helps explain why NASCAR drivers can survive horrifying end-over-end shunts at speeds approaching 200m.p.h. The NASCAR machine has a chassis built on the spaceframe principle with very heavy steel tubing mandatory. The shell is then welded on and stays production weight and even the doors are welded up for additional rigidity.

Roll cages are, of course, incorporated in Sports-Prototype chassis. Nigel Stroud of Mazdaspeed reported that the roll cage on his aluminium-based, composite '89 design contributed around 5% of the chassis rigidity: around 2–300 ft/lbs. He went on to point out that he felt that the regulations were at fault in that they allowed a chassis builder to mount a steel roll cage on a carbon composite chassis. In his view this combination of two incompatible materials would create weak points at the junctions of the steel and the composite.

On the subject of titanium roll cages, Stroud pointed out that if a car rolls and spills fuel, the situation is potentially very dangerous since titanium sparks more than ordinary steel (as shown by the titanium skid plates on the underside of Grand Prix cars). On a Sports-Prototype the fuel filler is usually next to the roll cage: if the car overturned the fillers are likely to be next to the contact point and there would thus be a high probability of ignition.

Seat and Seat Belts

The need for comfortable, effective seating is discussed elsewhere. The seat should be unpadded with the right degree of support and ideally should fit like a second skin. Perfect fit can be achieved via moulding with a special two-part, self-forming foam. Of course, it must be moulded with the driver sitting in the correct position and fully kitted out. The foam can be used as the actual seat or as a mould for a fibreglass seat. The danger of using the foam itself is that it is polyurethane, and thus gives off a very toxic gas should it burn.

In all major racing categories drivers have their own individually moulded seats which are light enough to enable them to be changed in a few seconds and this is of particular advantage in Endurance racing. The set-up of a car shared by two or more drivers is necessarily a compromise and the driver's own seat makes the cockpit more 'user friendly'. An uncomfortable driver cannot concentrate fully and will soon tire.

The production-based car can employ any number of proprietory seats but still there is a strong argument for an unpadded model, which is rare. However, it might well be possible to produce a foam moulded insert for a proprietory seat shell. Both moulded seat and shell must be securely fixed to the chassis, though. Also, the seat belt must be mounted to the chassis rather than the seat. Ideally, there should be 'progressive collapse' in the event of a major impact, whereby the belt brackets tend to bend the mountings under great stress rather than rip out. Clearly, if the brackets rip out the belt is useless.

In fact, seat belt is a misleading term: we are talking about a harness which must be six point. The seat belt, like the crash helmet, will deteriorate with time. It should likewise be replaced at least every two years. For that reason surplus belts are unwise. It is wise to buy the best available. As Allan Staniforth says in his *Race and Rally Car Source Book*: 'buy the best you can afford, not because the cheaper ones are weaker or are going to break, but because the more expensive ones have much better and simpler locking and adjustment devices on them. It not only saves a lot of messing about threading yourself in

The seat belt and the all important seat belt buckle. Rapid release can save a life…

and out, but may just be vital to getting you out in a hurry if something awful happens.'

Six point harnesses are mandatory for the major single seater formulae, and in prototype racing where the driver likewise is in a semi-reclined position. The regulations require two shoulder straps, an abdominal strap and twin crotch straps. The latter are vital in this application to prevent 'submarining': the effect of the driver sliding beneath the abdominal strap in a heavy frontal impact. Sadly, the worth of a six point harness only became apparent after Jochen Rindt's fatal accident at Monza in 1970.

The first racing harnesses were adapted from aircraft systems. They became widely used in competition in the United States during the Sixties and their use was heavily championed by Jackie Stewart in Europe after his participation at Indianapolis.

Tests have shown that, properly restrained, the human body is capable of withstanding enormous deceleration forces – close to 50g – without injury. However, the necessary degree of restraint of head, chest, arms and shoulders, is such that it would be impractical for a racing driver. The systems used by Grand Prix drivers in the Eighties were less restrictive and were reckoned to be capable of allowing the body to withstand up to 20g without injury.

A harness system is a very simple piece of equipment in basic form, the straps made from polyester webbing. The shoulder straps should be as wide as is practical and comfortable and are often worn with additional padding. On impact the driver's upper torso is likely to be pitched forward against the shoulder straps: the wider these are the more evenly the load will be spread – thin straps could cause additional injury by the opposite effect.

Under impact the webbing will stretch and this is not necessarily undesirable. However, as it will dissipate energy, it should be noted that a harness fitted in a purpose-built racing car is likely to have relatively short straps to avoid excessive stretch. In an adapted production car the harness system is likely to be anchored on the floor pan behind the driver's seat by long straps which will stretch further, increasing the risk of contact with the steering wheel or suchlike.

The most important part of any system is the buckle mechanism: a harness is worthless if the buckle should

Lauda usually was Boss. Wide straps can minimise injury and are another way of making money!

burst open under impact or fail to open afterwards as the driver tries to make his escape. Most buckles are of the twist type, requiring the movement of a catch by a quarter turn, or less, to one side to release the straps from the central buckle. Some systems employ a central push button but this is felt to be less secure as this makes the straps easier to release accidentally.

The buckle is the most expensive part of the harness constituting over 50% of the cost of the full system. There is a lot to be said for a driver familiarising himself with the various systems available. In at least one case this has saved another driver's life. As Niki Lauda writes in his autobiography *To Hell and Back* of his fiery accident at the Nurburgring in 1976: 'my real saviour was Arturio Merzario who plunged into the flames with total disregard for his own life and unbuckled my safety harness...'

It later emerged that the crotch straps on the Ferrari's Klippan harness had not released and it was only Merzario's knowledge of how the buckle operated, having himself driven for Ferrari, that permitted Lauda's removal from his burning car before it was too late.

Harness systems are easy to fit when sitting in the car if driving an adapted production car or prototype: in single seaters their fitting and closure is usually only possible with outside help, due to the lack of space in the cockpit.

The harness must be worn as tightly as comfort allows to hold the driver in place when cornering under heavy 'g' load and also to hold him in place in an accident. Despite feeling locked rigid into the seat, under impact the body will naturally stretch out of the restrained position.

Shoulder straps must be parallel over the driver's shoulders but may converge to a single mounting point – not practical in a single seater but often used in an adapted production car. Single seaters and Prototypes usually have the shoulder straps mounted on individual anchorage points, for example on top of the central fuel tank. The abdominal strap must also have two fixing points, usually the sides of the cockpit, while the crutch straps are also required to have two fixing points, usually on the floor and cockpit sides. The anchorage points are crucial: if the harness is not attached correctly to the chassis the system will be of no use whatsoever.

The individually
tailored seat is
preferable, wherever
space allows.
Unpadded is safest.

Steering

Invariably the competition car is steered through a rack and pinion system whereas a kart has direct steering. Ace kart racer Roger Williamson went motor racing with a modified Ford Anglia which he converted to direct steering. He found the quick, sharp response advantageous – until he over-cooked it. Then his steering reactions became over-reactions multiplying the error. Faced with that response problem Williamson resorted to conventional rack and pinion steering. Some sort of reduction is essential.

The difference between the number of teeth on the pinion to which the steering column is attached and the number of teeth on the steering rack is the steering ratio. This is typically in the region of 8:1, though it can vary widely. The response derived from a given rack ratio is influenced by the length of the steering arms (extending ahead or behind the kingpin), while desired response is in accordance with driver preference and the type of circuit. The size of the steering wheel must also be taken into account while the 'feel' imparted by a steering system is further influenced by the feedback given by the front tyres and the effort required to turn them. The steering weight is again influenced by the steering ratio.

Shorter steering arms make for quicker but heavier steering while steering effort is further influenced by the car's weight, its downforce and the front suspension geometry, and in particular the amount of caster angle. Front wheel caster provides a self-centring effect at the expense of heavier steering, but also helps keep the car true in a straight line at high speed and pulls the wheels back straight exiting a turn. King pin inclination and offset also influence the steering as well as handling characteristics. One aim of kingpin geometry is to achieve so-called centre point steering whereby an imaginary line drawn through the pin intersects with the centreline of the tyre on the road. Centre point steering is light and without 'kick back' through the wheel.

Akermann steering means that the inner wheel turns more sharply than the outer wheel in recognition of the fact that it is on a tighter radius. However, given that

A well designed modern racing steering wheel affords good grip and a clear view of the key gauges.

competition tyres work through a slip angle rather than following the geometric curve traced by the car the case for Akermann is less clear cut. Its use is a question of tyre performance, grip and handling rather than a direct steering influence.

Bump steer means that any rise or fall of either of the front wheels causes it to alter the way it is pointing without the steering wheel moving. It is caused when the rack and pinion is in the wrong place or is of the wrong length given the front suspension design and it is another factor which is considered in the companion Race Tech volume 'Competition Car Suspension' by Allan Staniforth.

A car should be driven in a smooth, relaxed manner that is unspectacular to watch. Driver hand and arm movements should be economical and ace drivers always look unflustered – a flailing of hands and arms is a sure sign of a no hoper. To be able to drive smoothly and economically the driver will require an acceptable ratio, good feel and a reasonable, preferably light steering effort. Steering which is light and easy will greatly reduce driver fatigue. Very heavy steering leads to consideration of power assistance but this extreme is rarely encountered in racing. Ligier toyed with power assisted steering for its radical and unsuccessful 1988 Grand Prix car, inconclusively. Power assistance adds weight to a car and costs steering feel.

Steering failure is rare as the rack and pinion system is essentially simple and reliable. A typical unit normally uses a cast magnesium housing enclosing a machined steel shaft incorporating the pinion teeth and splined to accept the steering column and the rack bar itself, machined from a robust steel rod. The rack is threaded to accept clevises at each end, these picking up the tie rods and locked via a nut. The pinion shaft will be carried in bearings, the rack in bronze bushes and there will be rack stops to limit travel in each direction. There will also be a pinion adjustment facility and a rack follower to set the gear lash between rack and pinion teeth. This follower – a spring loaded bush pressing against a flat at the back of the rack – also ensures the pinion cannot jump a tooth on the rack. Adjustment should be checked frequently and the bushes and bearings need to be regularly lubricated. The rack must be free in operation.

The tie rods between the rack and the steering arms are

simple tubular structures with rod end attachments. Adjustment of the outer rod end – threading it in or out – alters rod length for toe in/toe out. Both rods must be the same length and the rod ends must be watched for wear. Tie rods, steering arms and the steering column are vital chassis components since failure means loss of control. Regular inspection of all fasteners involved in the steering system is an important safety procedure.

The steering column is bolted over the pinion shaft splines and is often fitted with a universal joint at the pinion end. This must be a high quality joint to avoid the possibility of failure. The column runs in bearings and should be two piece incorporating a sliding sleeve joint to allow for adjustment of length and angle to suit a given driver and to make it collapsable in the event of an accident. A flange welded to the top of the column allows for the steering wheel to be securely attached with bolts. The wheel can be attached via a quick release hub which not only makes getting in and out easier but may be vital in the removal of a driver in the event of a shunt.

Since the steering system contains a number of joints there is a danger of 'stiction'. It only takes one tight joint, which might be in a front upright, a tie rod or supporting the column, to produce an unpleasant wooden feel. Staniforth says: 'a personal test and yardstick is that with the vehicle jacked up at the front you should be able to turn the steering wheel from lock to lock with the little finger bending the joints sideways. If your finger protests at this, the steering is too tight and will have to be dismantled one joint at a time until the trouble is found. If the stiffness is left uncured, it is capable of masking a load of other problems, virtues or vices as well as any meaningful driver feedback'.

Steering wheel type is largely a matter of driver preference, provided that a high quality make is employed to ensure integrity in the event of an accident. The worst wood rim type which could splinter in an accident has faded away in recent years.

Suspension

Race cars need high downforce for maximum cornering potential and high downforce invariably implies stiff suspension settings. The downforce pushes the car towards the track surface with a force that can be up to three times its own weight and the aerodynamic appendages that create that force need to be run at a consistent angle of attack for maximum effectiveness and predictable performance. The result is that these days there can be less than 1" of wheel travel and tyre wall flexibility is at least as significant as the springs and dampers in providing the suspension movement. Unfortunately such harsh suspension gives the driver an uncomfortable ride, and that increases fatigue.

In the early Eighties Colin Chapman designed a ground effect car that fed its aerodynamic loads directly into the wheel uprights, to full effect. This was the so called twin chassis car which isolated the monocoque and running gear from the coachwork, the latter of course including ground effect underbody and wings. Since the coachwork was connected directly to the uprights the rest of the chassis could be relatively softly sprung to give the driver an easier time.

Aside from a more comfortable ride, the twin chassis Lotus 88 promised another leap in the spiral of increasing cornering speed thanks to the direct loading of the uprights. The concept of mounting wing support struts directly to the uprights – an arrangement maximising hub and wheel loading and cornering speed – had been banned back in the late Sixties on the grounds of safety. By the same logic the Lotus 88 was illegal, and it was rejected from World Championship participation.

Suspension movement is minimal on modern Grand Prix cars, hence kerb hopping causes wheel lifting.

The Lotus 88 concept was heralded by Chapman as an answer to the conflicting requirements of driver comfort and aerodynamic performance but this was never put to the test. The possibility remains that in practice the conventional part of the chassis would have ended up harshly sprung. For example, soft springing might have promoted undesirable weight transfer. It seems the only sure resolution of the conflict is computer control of wheel movement and the 'Active Suspension' Lotus 99 raced by Ayrton Senna in 1987 gave its driver a far easier time over bumps than a conventional car.

Lotus Active-type and other computer controlled suspension systems come in many forms, some concerned purely with control of ride height and few of which have yet to be developed for racing. At the time of writing such systems are restricted to teams with large development budgets. A full discussion of the subject appears in the companion Race Tech series book, Competition Car Suspension by Allan Staniforth. Computer control of roll bar settings and damper movement are less exotic and bolt-on systems may be just around the corner.

Generally, racing cars employ progressive rate springing to increase stiffness with load input. In essence, the harder the car is driven, the harder the suspension becomes. As it travels faster its suspension stiffens up, reducing pitch and roll changes as the downforce climbs with speed. The anti roll bar linkage can be arranged so that the bar is worked increasingly hard as the springing stiffens. The roll bar's job is to limit roll, in doing which it acts like an extra spring and also causes weight transfer from inner to outer wheel which at the rear is not in the best interest of traction. For this reason not all racing cars run rear bars.

Spring and damper settings are generally impossible to re-adjust by the driver during the course of the race, though in the Fifties Mercedes Benz fitted a cockpit control to allow the driver to adjust the rear torsion bar setting once the fuel load had dropped to a certain level. However, cockpit control of anti roll bar strengths is commonplace. This allows the driver to evaluate different settings during qualifying and to compensate for varying track conditions or altered tyre characteristics.

An anti roll bar that is easily adaptable for cockpit control is one which has a blade adjustment facility. This means that one arm takes the form of a blade which is rotated through 90 degrees to give varying degrees of stiffness. Clearly, when the blade is horizontal it is a lot easier to bend it than when it is vertical. The rotating blade can be made cockpit adjustable via a simple cable control. The blade system has been criticised as the blade (sometimes twin blades) appears to act as an unwanted undamped leaf spring. Nevertheless, the system is widely employed by leading designers. The TWR team devised a system whereby each of its rear suspension upper wishbones had its forward leg leading directly into a blade on the opposite side of the wishbone pivot. The wishbone pivots were well inboard over the transaxle and two short blades met over the longitudinal axis of the car. Their ends were linked by a pair of rod ends, and that was the extent of the anti roll bar!

From the safety point of view, most suspension components are vital in the sense that failure is likely to cause a shunt. Suspension failure is all too common and sometimes indicates a part that is inadequate given the suspension loading, which can go very high in the case of cars employing effective underwings. Careful design and construction as well as proper preparation are essential to ensure a car stays on the road. In this sense the driver is at the mercy of the engineers – and where engineers are taking aerodynamic loading into new realms the driver might well be in the lap of the gods.

When a race car creates enough download to run upside down on the ceiling – as is the case, for example, with a modern Sports-Prototype at speeds in excess of 130/140m.p.h. – it is really a low flying airplane and the driver's job in testing a new design can be every bit as hazardous as that of the test pilot. An example: the accident that befell Grand Prix pilot Thierry Boutsen at Rio testing in 1989. His Williams suffered suspension failure, apparently due to suspension loading taking an unexpectedly high leap thanks to off season improvements in aerodynamic performance. Although uninjured, Boutsen was shaken up enough to lose driving performance in early races but he later bounced back and won the mid season Canadian Grand Prix.

Telemetry

In 1975 the Goodyear tyre company of Akron, Ohio commenced its Vehicle Dynamics Programme with the intention of bringing a more scientific approach to motor racing. For the next two Grand Prix seasons Dr Karl Kempf, working on a consultancy basis, constructed mathematical models of the pneumatic tyre and specifically the Formula One racing tyre. Kempf carried out numerous experiments with teams using Goodyear tyres, collecting the necessary information by means of a compact onboard computer system. Concurrent advances in the micro miniaturization of computer hardware allowing the first meaningful use of such systems. Previously onboard computers had been experimented with but enormous weight penalties resulted as the constituent parts weigh several hundred pounds while in addition to their physical size would compromise the aerodynamics and weight distribution of the car, making the data collected of limited use.

By 1975 Kempf was able to fit the cars under test with a computer recorder weighing only 30 lbs which would measure and record a variety of parameters critical in the construction of tyres such as pitch and roll angles, down-force and G-forces. The information collected was to prove surprising to many racing car designers as for the first time they were able to see in an interpretable form the on track behaviour of their designs rather than relying solely on theory and interpretation of the car by the driver.

Fifteen years later, at the beginning of the 1990s, for a Grand Prix team to be without some form of on board computer system would be unheard of. The systems in use now in the Grand Prix pitlane monitor a wide range of parameters from functions within the engine to suspension deflection and tyre temperatures. The availability of transmitters capable of sending and receiving high quality signals has resulted in the use of telemetry systems, whereby a car can be kept under constant observation by its on board computer and the information within transmitted back to the receiver in the pits, even in the heat of battle on the track.

A Honda Grand Prix engine is always linked to the pits via telemetry - the engineers constantly monitor its progress.

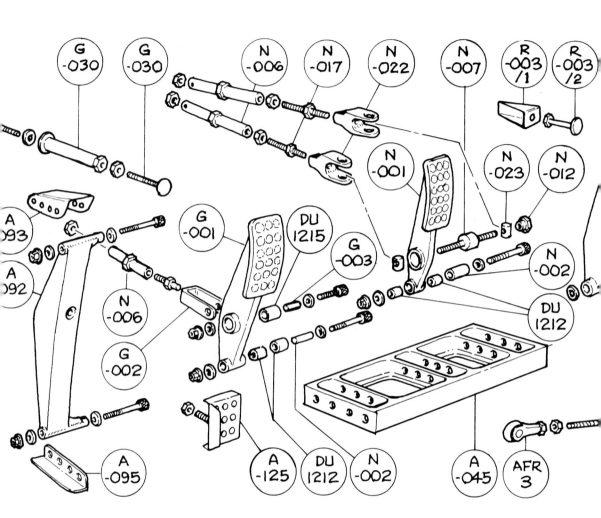

Throttle

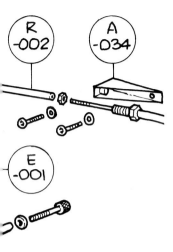

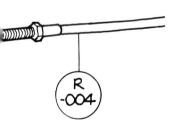

A stuck throttle amounts to a personal invitation to inspect the scenery, one that is likely to be very difficult to refuse. That should be reason enough to provide special attention to the linkage between the accelerator pedal and the engine slides or butterflies. The slide or butterfly shafts must be true and there should be two or more return springs of high quality. Cable is generally preferred over rod linkage to the pedal to allow for any engine movement and for sheer practicality. If the cable can take compression and the throttle pedal has a toe hook, the driver should be able to reject an invitation made by a sticking shaft or failed return spring.

Attention to the throttle linkage can pay dividends aside from the safety aspect. Checking for full throttle can be the cheapest of all tune-ups. The throttle pedal movement should be carefully synchronised to the engine throttle movement. A linkage can be designed for a slower ratio at high r.p.m. to give better feel and thus better control under power, and this is worth considering.

A failed throttle linkage is one of the most infuriating reasons for retirement. A proper stop on the pedal will avoid putting strain on the cable nipples. With reliability and safety in mind, the springs should be regularly changed and spare springs and cable should always be to hand. The cable should be checked for signs of wear and chafing at frequent intervals. It should have been very carefully installed so as to avoid the danger of chafing. Tight bends are not on, and nothing should be able to rub against it.

The pedals of a typical Sports-Prototype. Floor mounting is best in ergonomic terms.

*Flame resistant
underwear is an
essential element of
an effective set of
protective race
clothing.*

Underwear

When choosing racewear, careful consideration should be given to the fit. If loose-fitting overalls are worn, they will trap a valuable insulating layer of air inside and, most importantly, will allow underwear to be worn comfortably underneath for extra protection.

One of the major findings of the Jim Clark Foundation report published in the early Seventies was the necessity to wear multiple layers of protective clothing against fire. 'A great number of drivers wear just a coverall without flame-proof underclothing. It must be stressed that this is most undesirable', the report noted.

Normal underwear – cotton briefs and a cotton tee-shirt – is often worn under the race underwear for comfort, otherwise the flame resistant material might chafe the skin. Woollen socks are similarly worn under Nomex socks for comfortable feet. Wool is one of the most fire resistant of all natural fibres. Nylon or dyed material for socks or underwear is a danger, nylon melting under high temperature, dye causing blood poisoning should it enter the bloodstream through an open wound.

In a letter to *Autosport* in May 1989, Mike Theobald of Advanced Wear and Safety warned of the potential danger of cotton tee-shirts, saying: ' . . . one of the most important parts of racewear is flame retardant underclothing. Different underwear varies in comfort and protection yet drivers seem to find a cotton tee-shirt favourable. This is a most dangerous practice. Fibres in the tee-shirt will continue to burn long after the source of the flame has been removed from it, whereas a flame retardant cloth is self-extinguishing. This may mean that, in a cockpit fire, the tee-shirt next to your skin will go on smouldering.'

Theobald also highlighted the danger of scalding through sweat on the skin becoming heated. Theobald commented: 'In a case some years ago, the driver's race suit had not been touched by the flames, yet when his clothing was removed several layers of skin came away because the heat had turned his sweat to steam.'

Gerhard Berger, who survived the short inferno at

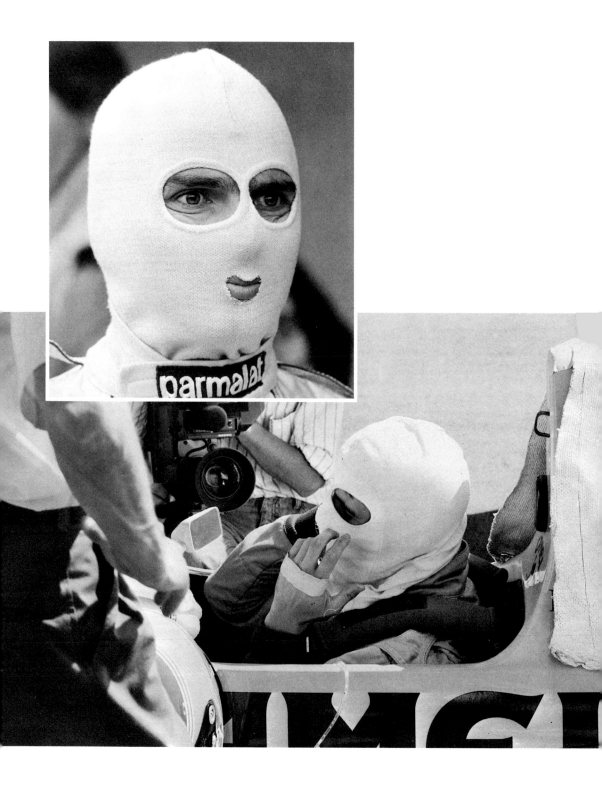

Imola in 1989 when his Ferrari crashed early in the San Marino Grand Prix, admits that the previous season he had worn a cotton tee-shirt instead of flame retardant underwear. He changed his view following a fiery shunt suffered by his friend Kris Nissen. At Imola Berger was wearing a four-layer OMP racesuit, comprising three inner layers of knitted Nomex, an outer layer of Nomex 3 over a layer of knitted Nomex underwear. In addition he had long Nomex socks and a double layer knitted Nomex balaclava and Nomex gloves.

Separate long underwear traps a further layer of air, providing a barrier to heat transfer as well as additional flame resistance. As with race suits, underwear must be tested to ISO 6940 and must be marked to this effect in a prominent position.

Flame retardant underwear should cover the wearer from ankle to wrist to neck. Given that the most vulnerable points in a fire are the ankle, wrist and neck, further protection there is vital. A high polo-type neck on the underwear gives added neck protection, as does a balaclava, which is required by FIA regulations to have been tested to ISO 6940 and to be made of at least two layers of flame retardant material. A helmet bib can offer further protection. Socks are also tested to ISO 6940 and must be of calf length. (Gloves are covered in a separate section.)

All such considerations and precautions could be compromised in an accident by something as simple as the wearing of jewellery. After all the efforts and expense of protective clothing, nasty burns through heat transfer could result from the wearing of rings, medallions and even wristwatches.

Under-clothing must not stop at the shoulders. A flame resistant balaclava is an essential safety item.

Visors and Goggles

In the pioneer days of motorsport, racing took place on unsurfaced roads and goggles were a vital part of a driver's outfit, enabling him to see through the clouds of dust thrown up by the competing cars. As surfaces improved, speeds increased and eye protection was necessary against the effects of a high-speed blast of air into the driver's face.

Racing goggles were initially those used by aviators. They set strong shatterproof glass, later plastic, in padded frames which were held onto the helmet (or, more likely in the early days, the head) by an adjustable strap. During a long race it was quite likely that the goggles would become covered in grime and as a precaution against this a spare set was often hung around the neck.

In wet weather goggles were troublesome in that they misted up and were difficult to clear. Indeed, some drivers dispensed with them altogether, preferring to race with rain lashing into their face rather than with vision compromised by condensation on the lenses of their goggles. A later, less radical and more comfortable solution to the problem was the use of a helmet visor. Effectively a large, single lens, the visor was easier to keep mist-free, since ventilation was far superior. Early visors were made of thin, transparent plastic and were fixed onto the helmet by straps or webbing. The Sixties brought attachment by press-studs to the helmet and in some cases visors that could be raised and lowered on pivots.

The problem of misting returned with the growing use of full-face crash helmets. In inclement conditions lack of ventilation can cause condensation to form inside a visor. Many techniques of preventing this have been recommended over the years, ranging from rubbing the inside of the visor with a piece of raw potato to the use of proprietary anti-misting sprays. One such was Vari-Clear, a spray developed by NASA for its space exploration programme, production of which has ceased. The Griffin Company at one stage produced a visor with a heating element but the extra electrical connections required were awkward and a heat source a few

Goggles are rare in modern racing but are not by all means unknown, as this shot illustrates.

centimetres from the face was often found uncomfortable.

Visors marketed as having anti-mist properties have yet to be fully effective. Given that the trick is to allow air to circulate behind the visor without letting water in, some drivers seal the top of their visor to prevent rain running through the gap between visor and helmet and then hold the bottom of the visor open with wads of tank tape to allow air to circulate.

The modern range of Shoei crash helmets features a visor ratchet system which allows the visor to be opened by small incremental movements at the touch of an external lever. The visor is adjustable to seven pre-set positions which the manufacturer claims will clear and prevent fogging. The incorporation of an internal helmet ventilation system also helps.

During the 1972 French Grand Prix at Clermont Ferrand, the Austrian driver Dr. Helmut Marko was hit in the face by a stone thrown up by a fellow competitor's car. The stone smashed through his visor and caused an eye injury severe enough to end his promising career. As a result of this accident, urgent research was carried out into the strengthening of visors. Today a typical visor is made of Lexan. This material is flame resistant and extremely strong. Tests have shown that the Lexan visor is capable of withstanding a shotgun blast. In fact, the modern Lexan visor is probably stronger than the helmet to which it is attached. Also, as the Lexan visor is moulded into its final shape, it is as near optically perfect as is possible: in the past distortion would occur in visors bent and stretched from flat sheets.

Coloured visors are the subject of much debate, one opinion holding that anything other than clear diminishes vision. Dark-tinted visors are useful in bright sunlight but become dangerous in dark conditions. While single-seater drivers race visor down, drivers of enclosed cars often leave the visor up or may even remove it completely. Some wear visors cut back to just sufficient depth to carry a sponsor's sticker. The unfortunate Kris Nissen was wearing such a visor when he had his fiery accident in a Japanese Group C race in 1988 and he received facial burns as a result. There is much to be said for racing with the visor closed, even in a coupé.

For single-seat racing the visor is usually fitted with 'tear-offs', which are thinner transparent layers on top of the outer surface. Nowadays these are filaments of plastic held on by static electricity with lugs on the edge arranged to allow removal in a predetermined order. In the past, thin rigid plastic strips were attached by tape and it was such an arrangement that proved to be the downfall of Chris Amon while leading the 1971 Italian Grand Prix. Amon tugged at one of the tear-offs and off came the whole visor. The blast of air in his eyes made it impossible to continue without a replacement and that cost him the race.

The bubble visor - popular back in the Sixties. This is the late Richie Ginther.

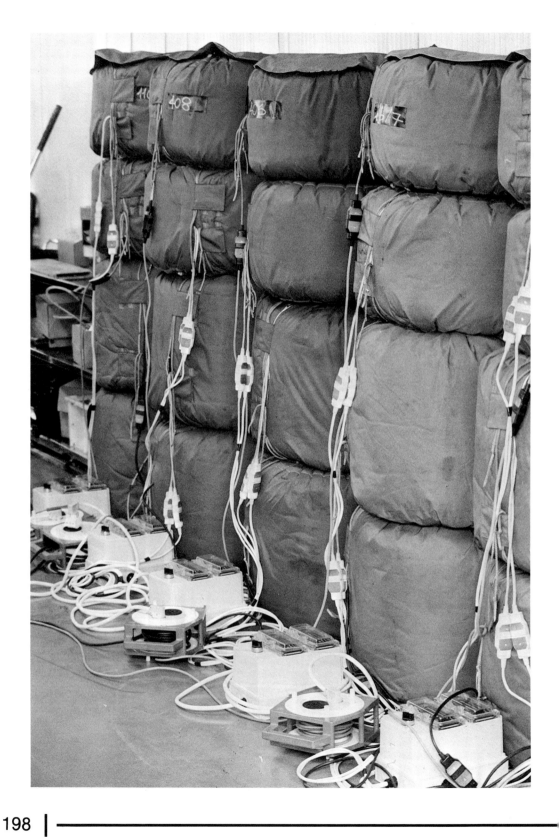

Wheels and Tyres

A car is kept on the road by four small patches of rubber. How that rubber is treated by the driver influences the grip it can produce, and serious abuse can lead to blistering which, in turn, can lead to a blow-out. Tyre temperature is the key consideration. A tyre will not work properly until it has reached a given temperature (and too many incidents are caused by drivers pushing too hard on insufficiently heated tyres). From the given temperature, there will be a range within which the tyre will work, beyond which it will go off, or blister.

Brake failure, vital steering or suspension component failure and wheel or tyre failure are the major causes of a car leaving the track of its own volition. Mechanical failure is sudden and essentially unpredictable, as often is a blow-out or instant puncture. However, a normal puncture can be identified by tyre pressure sensor, as developed for Group C racing, and this will also catch the slow puncture that is leading towards a blow-out through a steady build-up of heat.

A puncture is particularly dangerous on the Mulsanne straight at Le Mans. A leaking tyre can be kept up by centrifugal force until a cornering load is put through it: on the Mulsanne that load comes in the flat-out kink. The tyre collapses at a speed in excess of 200 m.p.h. and the inevitable result is a massive shunt. Ask John Sheldon (Aston Martin Nimrod) or Win Percy (TWR Jaguar). The Mulsanne danger helped spur the development by TWR and engine management specialist Zytek of a commercially available tyre pressure sensor. This followed the earlier co-operation between Porsche and Bosch in the production of a sensor that felt the actual pressure within a tyre through the wheel rim. It required special rims, which Bosch could not make available to TWR or other competitors.

The TWR/Zytek system, developed in the late Eighties, was based on the premise of an infra-red heat scanner 'reading' the surface of the tyre, the continually monitored heat reading indicating running pressure. The scanner was an expensive optical device (applied in a variety of fields) which resembled a video camera lens and was

Once the first few corners of a race highlighted skill as drivers grappled with low, low grip. Now tyres can be hot from the off.

positioned only fractionally off the tyre surface. The so-called 'Heat Spy' indicated the condition of the tyre with steadily rising temperature a symptom of dangerous pressure loss which was indicated via a warning light on the dashboard. The driver could also call up temperature readings for individual tyres on a combined Zytek digital fuel consumption and tyre temperature read-out.

The heat spy logged tyre temperature on a continual time basis, providing very valuable information for the tyre technicians. For the driver, the temperature readings could be useful in qualifying, allowing him to lean on his tyres while making sure they didn't get too hot and consequently go off.

The speeds reached on the Mulsanne are well beyond the capability of a 'run flat' tyre, but in 1989 Michelin was developing a run flat rally tyre with a 100 m.p.h. capability: at that speed it was claimed to be capable of lasting 30 miles. The so-called ATS run flat tyre was at first used by the Lancia rally team on slower events, but the high-speed version, at the time of writing, was scheduled for a late season introduction. The ATS system saw the tyre contain a foam compound filling which automatically expanded in the case of a puncture, replacing lost air and maintaining most of the pressure. Normal Lancia tyre pressure was in the region of 2.0 bar and the high speed version of ATS increased the pressure obtainable with the foam from 1.3 to 1.7 bar.

Two ton, 200 m.p.h. NASCAR stock cars run special tubes – so-called 'safety liners' – but otherwise racing tyres are generally tubeless. For a long while tyre manufacturers and others have experimented with various 'goos' which are applied to the inside of the tyre. Like thick glue, the goo is pushed outward by centrifugal force and tends to plug any small hole.

Competition tyres are invariably run with a bead retention system. Keeping the bead in place on the rim helps the driver maintain control in the event of a puncture. The retention can be achieved either by a hump incorporated in the rim to block bead shifting, or safety bolts. Safety bolts are screwed into the tyre wall through the rim. The disadvantage of the bolt is the obvious problem of sealing.

Retention of the bead helps minimise the impact of a puncture, and the low pressure run by tubeless racing tyres tends to discourage the sudden blow-out. Low

Reynard disc-type wheel for improved aerodynamics without compromising brake cooling. The wheel is cast thus, unlike BBS which has detachable inserts.

pressure doesn't stress the tyre carcase as much as high pressure and does not escape through a minute hole so quickly. That means the tyre is less likely to puncture on impact and deflates more slowly. On the other hand, contemporary racing tyres are of light construction and thus more prone to damage.

Tyre damage can be caused by stones picked up in the paddock, so careful attention must be paid towards ensuring the car always goes out with clean tyres. Punctures can also be caused by leaks from safety bolts, loose or damaged valving and improper wheel mounting. The valving must be regularly checked and valve caps must be used. The beads must be properly sealed and the entire wheel and tyre should be tested for leaks.

Wheel loss tends to be far less dramatic than a blowout, particularly where a car is very stiffly sprung. It is not uncommon for such a car to tricycle back to the pits for a replacement wheel. Porsche Group C cars had a spate of wheel losses in the mid-Eighties which for a while were mysterious. The lost wheels had, after all, had the runaway centre nut torqued to the correct setting. However, the problem was cured by a larger bore air line: though the guns employed had been achieving the required torque setting, they had clearly not done so in the required manner, since a bigger volume of air coming down the line did the trick!

Wheel failure is a more serious matter altogether and only tends to happen when the wheel is heavily loaded – in a corner. As with a blow-out, a trip into the scenery is the likely result. Magnesium wheels got a bad name in the early Seventies. Magnesium Elektron's Melmag racing wheels were among the first and suffered a number of failures before the hub was redesigned. A circular hub was replaced by a star-shape casting, with the points of the stars fitting inside the rim and keeping the wheel from collapse in the event of any failure. These modified Melmag wheels were more satisfactory but were later replaced by modular wheels, having magnesium centres with spun aluminium rims.

These days one-piece magnesium wheels are the ultimate for racing and wheel failure is, thankfully, a freak occurrence. The key points are that the wheel must be correct for the given application and that it must not be neglected: any wheel has a certain healthy life span, after which it is liable to show signs of cracking. An old wheel is

Zytek/TWR developed heat spy reads the temperature on the surface of the tyre.

a potential hazard, as is a wheel that has been through a shunt. Crack testing is essential. All wheels are subject to very heavy loading and steel, aluminium and magnesium wheels are all prone to fatigue. Regular visual inspection and annual crack testing are called for. Proper preparation of suitable strength wheels is the key to wheel safety.

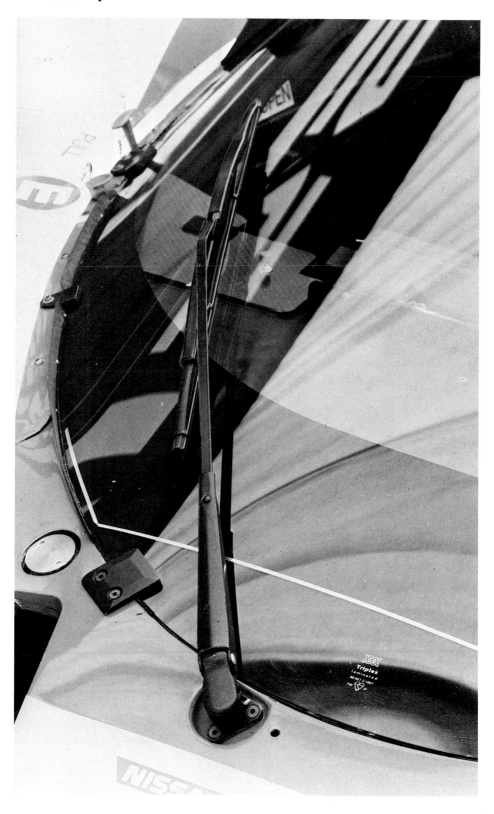

Windscreen and Wipers

Although the driver of a single seater tends to look over the windscreen, the screen is of major importance in minimising buffeting from the airflow. A driver cannot be expected to work well if his helmet is being mercilessly knocked around by the sort of aerodynamic forces generated at 100m.p.h. The height needed for this can conflict with the aim of seeing over the screen for good visibility. The transparent screen material will be curved and thus hard to see through, while it will be prone to collecting dirt. Looking over is the best solution, with careful screen shaping to deflect the air from the cockpit.

The height of the screen typically varies according to the circuit and speeds encountered. At Silverstone or Monza a high screen will be fitted to protect the driver from buffeting caused by the rush of air over the upper surface of the car. At a slow circuit such as Monaco where accurate placement of the car is paramount a low screen will be fitted.

In 1967 when the black art of aerodynamics was still in its infancy, Jack Brabham's Repco-engined BT24 chassis appeared for practice at Monza with a very high see-through streamlined windscreen fitted. The car proved no faster than in conventional form, and the driver complained of the curvature of the screen interfering with the forward vision. Thus, an interesting experiment was discarded. A similar arrangement was used through-out 1967 in Formula Two races by the Protos team. The Frank Costin-designed Protos had a slot cut in its screen to correct vision. Inconclusive results ensured that tall screens never caught on.

Plexiglas is commonly used for single seater screens and Sports-Prototype side windows, while full wind-screens require glass. Traditionally there have been conflicting claims for the safety of laminated versus toughened glass. Toughened glass is a sheet of glass that has been toughened to withstand the impact of stones and the abrasion of grit under the wiper. When a stone strikes it acts like a spring and bounces the stone back. However, in the face of a major impact it can collapse.

A laminated screen consists of two sheets of glass

Nissan windscreen wiper is adapted from production car issue. Note screen retention tabs.

separated by a plastic layer. A stone hitting the outer layer may cause a crack but it is likely to be small and should not affect vision. In the event of a major impact the laminated glass should break up in a controlled manner. It is possible to have a combination of laminated and toughened, the inner layer being toughened. In the event of major impact this screen will break into small pieces which are not sharp, and many will stick to the plastic layer.

Laminated glass is compulsory for racing and rallying in most cases. Where screens are likely to need replacement – such as at Le Mans – they are often clamped rather than bonded in place. It is possible to use a heated screen to avoid the danger of misting. Sports-Prototype windscreens can be a problem at night. With the long, shallow curved screen there is a danger of the instruments being reflected up into the driver's field of vision. Careful attention to dashboard design and lighting is called for. Another possibility to avoid is that of poor wiper action at high speed. Unless a small, slim aerodynamic blade is employed the wiper might find itself struggling at very high speed, such as achieved at Le Mans and Daytona.

The Mazda Group C car was fitted with a Japanese-made laminated screen. The team experimented with screens containing a heated element but, given the life expectancy of one race, this was considered a somewhat expensive luxury. The screen was bonded and clipped into a separate carbon fibre frame which was then bolted onto the chassis as a sub-assembly. Typically, the side windows were made from Perspex. The wiper was driven by a single speed motor adapted from a Mazda road car. A metal lip attached to the arm of the wiper prevented high-speed lifting.

On its rival car Nissan used a British-made Triplex windscreen with a heated element which occasionally cracked the screen. Nissan's side windows were made from Lexan, which was found to be more beneficially flexible than Perspex. On the debut of the Nissan GC89 at Dijon the team encountered a serious problem with the fixing of its windscreen. In its original form the car had completed 7000 kilometres of trouble-free testing. During practice in France it was decided to add a small additional ventilation duct to feed air into the cockpit. Twenty-three laps into the race the screen flew out of its mounting. A replacement repeated the act later in the race.

Initially, chassis flexing was suspected to be the cause

but it was later established that the small change in internal air pressure caused by the additional duct was literally blowing the screen out from inside. The seating of the screen was too thin and was duly strengthened. The use of double-size locking clips also helped ensure there were no further such incidents at subsequent races.

The Nissan, like the Mazda, used a wiper adapted from a road car. A single speed motor operated the arm and blade which swept two thirds of the glass surface. To prevent the blade lifting off at high speeds a scollap on the wiper arm was used, and on occasion an aerodynamic lip at the bottom edge of the screen to lift air over the wiper.

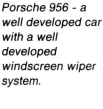

Porsche 956 - a well developed car with a well developed windscreen wiper system.

SPECIAL INVESTIGATIONS

COOL CAP
BRAKES
ELECTRICS

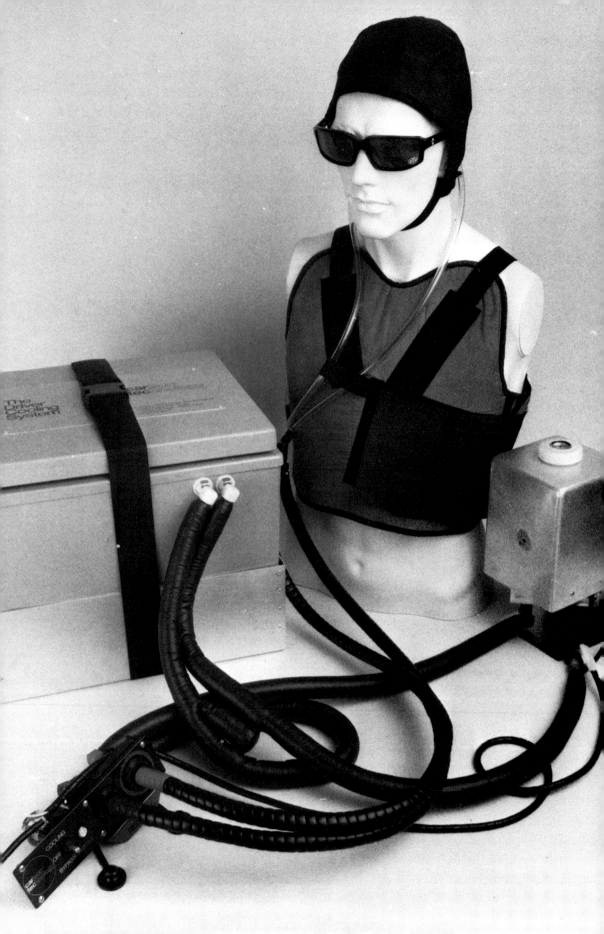

COOL CAP

Heat in the cockpit of a racing car has been a problem since racing began. However, in the pioneer days of the sport the drivers wore less in the way of protective clothing and were positioned higher up in the air stream, remaining relatively cool – at least while the car was in motion. As racing car design became more sophisticated and aero-dynamics and weight distribution were improved, drivers found themselves firmly in as opposed to riding on the car. And it was hot there.

Until the late Fifties, with a few exceptions, racing cars had a front mounted engine. Thus, the driver would be sitting astern of two major sources of heat: the engine and its cooling radiator. With the revolutionary change to mid-engined designs, the driver's lot became less uncomfortable. However, radiators remained front mounted and heat would still flow into the cockpit. Teams running spaceframe chassis were sometimes able to improve ventilation by removing side body panels, the method demonstrated on Stirling Moss's winning Lotus at Monaco in 1961.

The introduction of the monocoque-type chassis and a further lowered driving position with Colin Chapman's Lotus 25 in 1962 made cockpit cooling even more difficult. The shape of the car was intended to flow air over the cockpit area and to leave the driver free of wind buffeting. For races in hot climates lengths of hose would be seen attached to the chassis with the intention of feeding air into the cockpit. At the end of a hot race it was not unusual to see a driver having cold water poured over him, sometimes while still in his car!

Heat problems were somewhat alleviated in the early Seventies by the introduction of side mounted water radiators which made the cockpit a far more comfortable environment for the driver. However, around the same period advances in the design and use of flame retardant overalls would mean that even in conditions of extreme heat a Grand Prix driver would get into his car wearing up to five layers of protection with obvious effect on body temperature. The introduction of the full-face protecting crash helmet exacerbated the problem.

In the late Sixties NASA developed the head bladder method of cooling as a remedy to heat stress problems being encountered by military helicopter pilots during the war in Vietnam. A number of seemingly unexplainable crashes were found to have been caused by pilots blacking out from the excessive heat within their aircraft, a problem aggravated by the need to wear a close-fitting protective helmet. The solution devised by NASA concentrated cooling on the areas of the body most efficient at transferring heat, i.e. the head and neck. A cooling liner shaped to fit the head was sufficiently compact to be worn under the existing standard issue helmet.

At the 1978 Brazilian Grand Prix, Patrick Tambay blacked out as a result of the heat during the race. His McLaren M26 came to rest without harm. As a result of this incident Gary Knutson of McLaren Engines in Detroit, USA, asked engineer Dennis Carlson, who had been working for the team in his spare time, to devise a driver cooling unit for racing.

Carlson had been working with a NASA engineer on solar energy projects and contacted NASA for information on personal cooling. NASA's reply gave details of experimental work carried out at The Ames Research Centre, which had aimed to improve the system used in the Apollo moon landing programme and adapt it for use by helicopter pilots in Vietnam. The hood-shaped bladders were available from a proprietary manufacturer. Carlson then set about the design and construction of a suitable solid state refrigeration unit which would be compatible with the hood.

Working with McLaren Engines team manager Roger Bailey, Carlson had a system tested and fully operational by April 1978. Installed in the team's BMW 320i driven by David Hobbs, the system worked without a hitch throughout its first race, the IMSA championship round at Road Atlanta, as it did in subsequent events. When the BMW project ended, development continued with Ted Field's Interscope team running Porsche 935s. Absence of reliability problems enabled Carlson to concentrate on reducing the size of the cooler and increasing efficiency. In 1981 Carlson Technology Inc supplied its first customer, Bruce Leven, and it later sold a system to John Fitzpatrick.

At Sebring in 1982 the track temperature was measured at over 100 degrees F. Carlson systems were in use by Fitzpatrick and Ralph Kent Cooke, who kept wonderfully cool. The first IMSA win came at Mid Ohio in May '82 with Fitzpatrick driving and the following month 'Fitz' and Hobbs finished fourth behind the works Porsche 956s in their 935 at Le Mans. This was the Carlson system's

European debut and it operated faultlessly for the full 24 hours.

In 1983 the ice chest system was introduced. This was basically an insulated box which would be filled with ice immediately before the race, obviating the need for a heavy and power absorbing refrigeration unit. Using this system David Hobbs won the 1983 Trans Am championship. The refinement of placing an hermetically sealed capsule of frozen silica gell in the insulated box was used by Bobby Rahal in his Truesports March 83C to take Carlson's first CART win at Riverside when track temperatures reached over 130 degrees.

1984 saw the Carlson system finally in use in Formula One, the application for which it had been devised some six years earlier. Keke Rosberg won in the sweltering heat of the Dallas Grand Prix. In 1985 the system was introduced to the world of NASCAR and caught on fast, Bill Elliot scoring the first win. By 1986 Carlson Technology was involved in many areas of motorsport including rallying, hydroplane racing and powerboat racing.

By the beginning of 1989 the success of the cool cap system was such that saturation point had been reached in certain categories of racing. Further, the high quality and reliability of the systems sold led to a situation where a good proportion of Carlson's business came from maintaining and updating existing equipment, in addition to selling it to new converts.

As a result of its success in motor sport, Carlson Technology has found customers in a diversity of fields outside of racing. The cool cap has proved its worth in use by surgeons in operating theatres and most recently in the Nuclear industry. The order for the latter resulted from a company executive seeing the Carlson system explained in a special feature on a television broadcast of a NASCAR race.

THE SYSTEM

The Carlson Technology Inc. cool cap system comprises a shaped fabric hood, weighing approximately four ounces, formed from a number of small diameter tubular coolant channels. The channels act as the supporting structure, avoiding the need to incorporate additional tubing through which to flow the cooling fluid. The hood is connected to the cooling source via flexible plastic hoses fitted with dry break couplings.

Various methods of fluid cooling are employed; ice, silica gel in frozen capsule form and thermoelectric refrigeration and compressed freon gas. The fluid circulated through the system is usually a water and propylene glycol solution with additional wetting agent and antifungal ingredients. Propylene glycol is a commonly used thickener in hair shampoo and is ideal in a cooling system application in that in the event of leakage it is non-injurious to human skin. A 15% methanol component can be added to lower the freezing point of the solution. It is also possible to operate the system using plain water.

A magnetically coupled gear pump circulates the fluid at 12–15 p.s.i., this pressure required to expand the capillary channels in the cap and allow the solution to flow. The expansion improves contact with the wearer's head. The fluid reservoir and cooler unit can be mounted in any convenient position on a car. Sensibly this should be away from sources of heat; on a single seater it is usually in a side pod while in a Sports-Prototype the usual location is a sill of the monocoque.

The fluid temperature is adjusted by either mechanical or electronic thermostats or by an electronic timer which proportions the amount of time that the solution is exposed to the cooling source. Within the cooler unit the fluid is passed through a conductive metal coil immersed in the cooling medium. The frozen capsule and ice methods usually require replenishment after about an hour, which conveniently coincides with fuel stop schedules in prototype racing.

The insulated container should be securely closed to prevent spillage – as one unfortunate IMSA driver will testify, having had the uncomfortable experience of having a capsule escape into the cockpit and land in his lap, freezing certain delicate parts of his anatomy!

During the swelteringly hot conditions prevailing at the 1989 Phoenix Grand Prix, personal cooling systems again became a vital part of many teams' equipment. Since its introduction and subsequent success the Carlson system has spawned imitators. One of the rival systems, unlike Carlson's, circulated pressurised Freon gas. During the race morning warm-up, a driver reported feeling unwell. On further investigation a leak in his cooling skull cap was found and as a result the drivers were advised by the FISA doctor, Professor Sid Watkins, not to use personal cooling systems in the race. It was felt that an accumulation of fumes inside a driver's crash helmet could induce narcosis with obvious dangerous consequences.

A meeting of the FISA Safety Executive followed shortly and a ruling was made that cooling systems circulating Freon gas would be outlawed despite contrary arguments that any leakage would be safely vented away by the airflow of the car in motion.

Carlson itself had investigated the use of Freon, but had decided that it was too dangerous. Calculations had revealed that the cannister of gas necessary to operate a system would, if leaked into the atmosphere, require a dispersal area of 4,000 cubic metres. A crash helmet is barely one cubic metre. Questioned as to how the FISA ruling might affect his company's products, Dennis Carlson replied "The FISA restrictions were aimed at the use of pressurized containers of chloroflurocarbons, which can rupture violently and produce toxic and corrosive by-products. We don't believe our equipment will be affected by the FISA investigation."

Modern brake systems are well proven products capable of pulling 1000kg. cars from speeds in excess of 240m.p.h. to a stop within a remarkably short distance. Clearly, though a tremendous amount of energy has to be absorbed in the process. How much energy is involved in a given braking operation is a function of the weight of the car in question and the speed change made. However, not all the energy has to be absorbed by the braking system since the rolling resistance of the tyres, the frictional loss of moving parts of the vehicle and aerodynamic drag all lend a hand in the deceleration.

Of course, dragsters rely heavily upon air drag braking, releasing a parachute to help scrub off a quarter mile terminal speed that might well be in excess of 240m.p.h. Parachute-assisted braking is clearly impractical in most other automotive, and even aero applications, aircraft instead using retractable flaps. These flaps are built into the wing and are adjusted by the pilot. They are designed primarily to increase lift to allow shorter take-off and slower landing. Increased lift means increased drag and the flaps are used upon touchdown at the maximum drag setting – in other words vertical - to provide an air braking effect.

In the pioneering days of race car wings it was possible to adjust a wing's angle of attack to provide downforce under cornering without a significant drag penalty on the straight. Ferrari went one step further with its 1968 Can Am car, reviving the idea of an air-brake flap as used by Mercedes on its Le Mans cars of the mid Fifties. Thus, the six-litre Ferrari 612 had a large (1750 × 300mm.) wing mounted on posts over the roll bar adjustable between two positions via a button on the steering wheel plus three braking flaps: two small flaps built in to the trailing edge of the wing and a nose flap.

The air brake flaps were operated via a separate hydraulic system which was activated by pressure on the brake pedal. The nose flap was perforated for additional drag-creating turbulence having been copied directly from a French Caravelle aircraft's wing flap. However, it did not stay on the car for long since it was found to cause lurid pitch changes! Soon, of course, the authorities demanded that all aerodynamic appendages on racing cars be fixed when on the move.

Paul van Valkenburgh (2) has calculated that 10 - 20% of a car's braking performance comes from air drag on the body, the actual percentage depending on the shape presented to the air and the speed, for the drag force is a function of the square of velocity. In contrast, neither tyre rolling resistance nor frictional losses play a serious role, and along with aerodynamic drag these are factors that the engineer anyway wishes to minimise since they reduce acceleration. As far as possible therefore, the kinetic energy of the vehicle's intertia is converted to thermal (heat) energy via the braking system.

How much braking force will a given car produce? A number of factors contribute to the answer, not least of which is the driver's input. The force applied by the driver is multiplied by pedal leverage, in practice generally in a ratio between 4 and 6:1. This ratio is a comparison between the distance travelled by the pedal foot plate and the distance travelled by the rod actuating the master cylinder. Clearly, this is determined by the height above the floor pivot at which the actuating rod's take-off point is set.

Brake fluid is incompressible: it will transmit the force exerted on the pedal to the brake pads in a progressive manner. Further, pressure in a given system is equally exerted on all its surfaces. However, the relationship between the diameter of a master cylinder piston and the diameter of the associated caliper piston(s) is significant. Firstly, it governs how much the brake pedal moves. A bigger master cylinder used in conjunction with the same sized calipers tends to give a heavier pedal with less movement.

Further, alteration in the size of the caliper pistons affects the pressure on the pad backplates. However, such variations are totally beyond the scope of all but the manufacturer of the caliper. Similarly, other factors governing braking force that, generally speaking, are outside the scope of all but the supplier are the friction material co-efficient, the brake disc application radius and the tyre radius. Tyre sizes are rarely chosen with regard primarily to braking performance.

Thus, in answer to our original question, the braking force that can be developed is directly proportional to the amount of force applied to the pedal. Unless we are in a position to change caliper, disc or tyre sizes, or can substitute an alternative friction material with a higher co-efficient of friction, an increased braking force for a given driver input can only be produced by altering the pedal leverage ratio.

How much force do we need? This essentially depends upon the weight of the car and its tyre co-efficient. At least in sprint events, a driver should always supply a lot of pedal effort – otherwise he is likely wasting valuable lap time. And pedal pressure should not easily lock the wheels. At the other end of the spectrum is pedal effort that is inadequate for our needs, calling for power assistance. This has not traditionally been a problem with racing cars though AP did develop a servo system that was tested by Renault in 1981 on its pioneering turbo Formula One car. Turbo cars demanded more driver effort and the system was intended to reduce driver fatigue but its disadvantages were excess weight and a loss of pedal feel.

Pedal feel is an important consideration. Driver preference will be for either a little softness at the start of the pedal travel or for a shorter travel 'brick wall' pedal. Pedal feel is again influenced by the pedal leverage ratio and the size of the master cylinder. A higher pedal leverage ratio means longer travel (but improved leverage effect) while a larger bore master cylinder creates increased pedal resistance.

The braking force produced within a given system is distributed between the various wheels in accordance with the relative caliper sizes and the relative disc and tyre sizes. However, the load on each wheel is not fixed in this manner. Each wheel's tractive capacity varies constantly and at any given time the wheel with the least tractive capacity relative to its given braking force is the one that will lock.

Wheel load is influenced by a number of factors. Obviously the static weight and the distribution of masses is important, but weight transfer also plays a major role. The dynamics of weight distribution are influenced by the length of wheelbase, the height of the centre of gravity, even the suspension set-up employed. As is well known, under braking weight goes forward, loading the front wheels (and thus brake systems are generally designed for a forward bias). A car with a low centre of gravity and long wheelbase will experience less weight transfer. For example, the 'lay down' Brabham BT55 with its radically low driver and engine position and its unconventionally long wheelbase had superb braking by the standard of 1987 Formula One, all four wheels sharing the load well.

The aerodynamic split is another factor influencing dynamic tyre loading, while tyre friction co-efficients can vary front to rear further influencing the distribution of tractive capacity. The friction co-efficient is dependent upon tyre size, tyre characteristics and track conditions. In the wet the fronts are helping sweep a path for the rears and thus have a markedly lower co-efficient and will tend to lock up first.

The rear tyres can benefit from an engine braking force, though at low r.p.m. the brakes might have to pull the engine down which subtracts from the rear braking force. The often overlooked positive effect of engine braking was highlighted by the experience of the Porsche 917 Can Am car that pioneered turbocharging in international road racing. The 917 turbocar suffered an inevitable loss of engine braking and further stress was put on the braking system by the driver putting his foot on the throttle early, while his other foot was still on the brakes, in an effort to overcome the problem of turbo lag. Porsche found pad and fluid temperatures running too high for comfort and designed its own well finned calipers for superior heat dissipation.

The ideal would be to proportion the braking force between all four wheels so that at any given moment each wheel received force in proportion to its tractive capacity – its ability to transmit that force to the track. In practice this is impossible without a system such as ABS. The best that can be achieved via a conventional braking system is driver-adjustable front to rear proportioning.

Where there is a single master cylinder in the system it is necessary to limit the amount of hydraulic pressure fed either to the front, or more often the rear brakes via special valving. More potential exists when, as is usually the case in competition applications, the pedal operates twin master cylinders via a common balance bar. Dual system braking is often mandatory and certainly having separate systems for front and rear brakes is essential from a safety point of view, to ensure that a system failure does not mean total brake failure. Production car tandem systems are far less satisfactory than the side-by-side arrangement of master cylinders used in competition applications.

The two master cylinders are generally of the same size while the ratio of the sizes of the front and rear caliper pistons then influences the basic distribution of braking force front to rear. However, different sized master cylinders can be employed to the same effect while a bias bar can be introduced to fine tune front to rear proportioning. The bias bar is a straightforward method of altering the proportioning without having to change master cylinders or calipers. The bar receives the entire pedal force and distributes it between the two master cylinders which are positioned at either end of it. If the pedal input – the bar's pivot point – is at the centre of the bar the proportioning will be 50 – 50 and there are various ways in which the pivot point can be offset to provide a set amount of bias towards one cylinder or the other.

A very simple system is that which provides for the easy substitution of alternative bars, these drilled so as to offer varying degrees of offset. At the other end of the spectrum is the sophisticated system which provides for adjustment via a cable running from a control in reach of the driver. This not only saves time during practice, but if necessary allows the driver to alter the bias during a race, perhaps in the case of rain. Whatever type is used it has another vital function – it must self-lock after a certain amount of unequal movement, so that pressure is maintained in the undamaged brake circuit whether front or rear.

On the dry race track, brake proportioning should be such that both front and rear brakes lock up at just about the same time. However, the fronts should lock up just before the rears rather than the other way around to ensure stability. Front wheel lock up causes a tendency towards understeer which the driver can hope to combat. Even if sliding straight on with the front wheels shrouded in tyre smoke, his only hope is to ease off the pedal, add some more lock and scrabble out of the situation. Rear wheel lock up promotes a more difficult to combat oversteering characteristic – quite possibly the car will slew sideways!

Broadly speaking, in a single seater it is better to flat-spot a front than a rear tyre since the flat will at least be visible and at the less heavily loaded end of the car. On the other side of the coin is rally driving on the loose. Here rear bias might be employed to encourage tail swinging oversteer. Indeed, rear bias is sometimes employed as a very crude fix for a race car that won't 'point'! Crippling the end of the car that's working well is clearly self defeating. Another sin, though not as serious, is running too much front brake bias – this is all too easily done. Again broadly speaking, significant brake bias either way is undesireable since it underworks one end of the car and thus diminishes the overall potential of the system.

Unless a driver is very sensitive, accurate fine-tuning of bias may be well nigh impossible without the help of trackside observers to report the onset of wheel lock. And wheel lock is a poor test since it is liable to flat spot the tyres. Clearly, plenty of testing is called for where experience is lacking. Cockpit control is not really intended for fine tuning in the heat of battle – that would be impractical – but it can prove invaluable for a rally driver switching from the loose to a tarmac section, or for a race driver compensating for a race which turns wet. In such cases a suitable degree of adjustment can be pre-determined in testing.

Testing is necessary to establish the right degree of brake cooling for a given circuit. As we have noted, brakes are designed to transform kinetic energy into heat energy and that heat has to go somewhere: the mass of the disc can only store a given amount. If excess heat is not properly dissipated from the disc and caliper the pads will exceed their proper operating temperature will fade and/or the fluid will boil and the brakes will then become spongy or non-existent.

The pads have a co-efficient of friction which rises rapidly with heat input until it reaches a given heat range, which may well be in excess of 1100 degrees centigrade. Operating within its range, the pad's co-efficient will stay constant. However, to exceed the heat range is to drop the co-efficient rapidly (hence the fade) and may well leave a permanent glaze. The fluid is in constant contact with the caliper and its piston and these can be running at over 500 degrees. Brake fluid cannot be designed to run much over 550 degrees and to exceed its boiling point is to cause air bubbles. These are compressible and thus take up pedal travel. Indeed, if the fluid boils the pedal may well go to the floor. As a further by-product of inadequate cooling, it is possible to suffer cracked discs. If a disc cracks apart, as with line breakage, the result is instant failure.

Clearly, it is necessary to cool both the disc and the caliper (and thus the fluid). On the other hand, over cooling can cause a loss of braking efficiency as well as wasted aerodynamic drag since the friction material is designed to work within a given temperature range.

However, cold brakes are only likely to be experienced in the rain. A special case is the three and a half mile long Mulsanne straight at Le Mans. Here brakes cool right down, then they are banged on hard for the Mulsanne corner. This sudden thermal shock has often caused problems of disc cracking and special discs are typically run at the circuit. Often these are characterised by thicker plates and a lack of cross-drilling.

It is important to remember that the co-efficient of friction between pad and disc varies with operating temperature. For effective and progressive braking the front and rear brakes should operate at similar temperatures and should reach their operating temperature at roughly the same rate. Carroll Smith emphasises this point (3), saying: 'This will keep the front to rear braking ratio constant during deceleration from very high to very low speeds and allow maximum utilisation of the braking system by the very sensitive driver. Damned few drivers are that sensitive, but I have worked with a few and it has been a pleasure. Achieving this balance – which is not to be confused with front to rear proportioning of braking effort or pad wear – is a question of more air to the fronts and/or less to the rears'.

Brake cooling is managed through the provision of brake ducting, which typically is altered from circuit to circuit. These days difficult-to-cool solid discs are rare: they are inadequate except for narrow tyred cars which cannot develop significant braking force. Modern cast iron ventilated discs have two plates sandwiching internal vanes. The disc takes the form of two paralell rings which are cooled by the internal vanes. Cooling air is directed to the eye of the disc – its inner edge – and is drawn in by the centrifugal pumping action of the vanes, which are designed to centrifuge the air out of the periphery of the disc. Often cooling air is also fed to the body of the caliper and sometimes wheels are designed so that cooling air flung out of the periphery of the disc is pumped out through the rim. Otherwise expelled air simply escapes as best it can.

Properly set up, with the right proportioning and cooling, the brakes ought to be able to enable the driver to hold all four wheels on the verge of lock-up from top speed to minimum speed throughout the duration of a race. In theory a tyre has its maximum traction at a point just short of lock up and thus conventional wisdom has it that a car stops faster with its wheels unlocked. However, van Valkenburgh (2) says, 'in practice, race tyres are so sensitive that a race car *may* stop in a shorter distance with all four wheels locked up. That's worth keeping in mind for the crucial emergency when loss of steering control is no problem – or is already lost'.

Brake systems are bolt-on parts which clearly need to be properly installed and set up. Such attention won't necessarily improve lap times but should assist car controlability and give the driver more confidence. Brake problems are now rare if bedding, proportioning and cooling are properly attended to. However, from time to time pad knock-off occurs. Porsche experienced this in its second season with the 917, its first big capacity sports-racing car. This powerful machine had run into brake heat dissipation problems in its first season in response to which Porsche inverted the pistons in the caliper. This kept the fluid further from the hot pad and created an air pocket between the pad and the fluid as well as minimising the contact area between the pad back plate and the piston. However, while reducing the heat transfer between pad and fluid it was found to cause pad knock-off: at the 1970 Daytona 24 hour race – the first race trial – the drivers complained of frequently having to pump the pedal.

The pad knock-off was accompanied by taper wear and both were blamed on a wobbling of the front discs caused by flexing of the stub axle or play in its bearings. Knock-off is normally caused by disc distortion or run-out for some reason. A new axle and hub system was designed and was fitted, untested, to the model for the following Sebring 12 hour race. It failed, giving the Ferrari 512 a rare taste of victory. Following that infamous defeat the hub assembly was redesigned and the quasi-works JW Automotive 917 team switched from the regular ATE to Girling brakes.

Fifteen years on, TWR did not have knock-off problems with the conventional AP braking system it ran on its Jaguar V12-engined Sports-Prototypes until it went IMSA racing. The IMSA GTP series is much harder on brakes than the Group C racing that TWR had previously experienced with its heavy (850kg.) and powerful (750b.h.p.) machine. Running in GTP exposed a problem that had been just under the surface. TWR mounted its conventional, cast iron curved vane AP disc on an aluminium bell in a manner that allowed it a little lateral float but did not allow it radial expansion. Radial expansion would therefore pull the bell, causing it literally to bell out which put the disc out of alignment. The harsh demands of GTP caused this to happen to the extent that pad knock-off became a problem. In response TWR had to design a clever dog drive that allowed a disc to expand without pulling its bell.

While Girling was strong in racing in the early Seventies it quit at the end of the decade, leaving AP/Lockheed and Brembo to supply discs and calipers for the endurance and Formula One arenas. However, since the 917 turbo days Porsche has furnished its many racing customers with its own calipers and latterly its own discs, the discs from an undisclosed sub contractor.

A typical conventional racing car system of the late Eighties was that fitted to the Pontiac-Spice Fiero GTP-L customer car for Camel Lights competition. This ran AP brakes and fluid and twin Girling master cylinders. The Fiero employed cast iron AP curved vane discs of 12.4" diameter and 1.1" width attached to aluminium bells via 12-1/4" UNF high tensile bolts. Each disc was stopped by a single aluminium AP four pot caliper with differential bore pistons. On each side of the disc, the two pistons had different sized bores to discourage taper wear, the leading piston being of smaller diameter. The caliper, rigidly bolted to the upright, carried Ferodo pads, either DS11 or 2459 compound, the latter a softer alternative that offered more bite with a corresponding increase in pad wear.

The copper-asbestos pad (with random fibre asbestos and copper particles) as typified by the Ferodo DS11 was traditional in racing until the arrival of the asbestos-free Pagid pad in Group C in the late Eighties. In the mid Eighties AP and Brembo supplied Ferodo pads while Porsche supplied Raybestos, an American alternative, for its customers. Meanwhile, Pagid of Essen, Germany got a foothold in racing through production race and rally cars and Formula Three single seaters. In 1987 it was adopted by Brembo and was thus used by the Richard Lloyd Porsche 962 team, which had switched away from Porsche brakes for its special honeycomb monocoque car. Lloyd gave Pagid its first World Championship victory at the 1987 Norisring meeting.

Pagid uses an organic material, carbon/graphite, with

only a small metal element. Different compounding produced three basic pads, the RS4 with a mu value of 0.45, the RS9 – 0.37 – and the RS7 – 0.33. The higher mu value implies a softer compound which fades at a lower temperature. Group C cars generally ran the RS9 pad.

Another major development in pad technology arrived soon after the Pagid asbestos free pad, the carbon-metallic pad produced by the American company Performance Friction. Still used with a conventional cast iron disc, the carbon metallic pad essentially consisted of a block of carbon impregnated with metal particles and boasting a mu value of 0.55. The super-successful Nissan GTP team of 1988 tried the product at Portland and stuck with it. Team Manager Ashley Page reported that the new pad provided a shorter stopping distance, with a good wear rate and good consistency. However, he warned that the bedding in procedure for both pads and discs was very important and that the pads were hard on discs. As he points out, that was to be expected – stopping more quickly generates more heat!

Carbon-metallic pads arrived in Group C the following season, pioneered by the Nissan and Aston Martin teams which used them at Le Mans without problems. At the same time, carbon-carbon discs and pads were starting to creep into Sports-Prototype racing having become firmly established in Formula One. The most obvious characteristic of the carbon-carbon brake is lack of weight. For a given heat storage requirement a carbon-carbon disc can be no more than two thirds the weight of a cast iron disc. In the Sixties Porsche toyed with beryllium discs which similarly saved weight, doing the same job as cast iron for a considerable saving of weight. However, they were horrendously expensive and gave off a poisonous dust: hardly a practical proposition away from the marque's project to produce a one off super-light hillclimb special.

In any case, the key advantage of carbon-carbon discs – carbon filaments sintered in a carbon matrix – is a markedly higher friction co-efficient with the bonus of improved heat characteristics. Carbon-carbon discs offer improved heat storage capacity with poorer conductivity (hence less heat transfer) and a significantly lower co-efficient of thermal expansion. Applied first to military aircraft, the new carbon-carbon brakes could operate at up to 1700 degrees centigrade whereas cast iron melts at 1500 degrees!

Originally developed for Concorde, the heat resistant carbon fibre reinforced carbon (or C.F.R.C.) discs were introduced to racing by Brabham. They offered an unsprung weight saving which could be as high as 25kg. with the bonus of reduced rotating mass. Lower mass means lower inertia: it is thus easier to accelerate and brake and will follow a road surface better. In practice lessening the unsprung, rotating mass was a somewhat marginal gain but the overall weight saving was significant, as, more importantly was the higher co-efficient of friction (mu of around 0.5 as against 0.3) of carbon-carbon discs with matching pads. Carbon-carbon discs promised lower pedal effort yet significantly greater deceleration.

Development of carbon-carbon brakes suitable for racing was a laborious process. The brakes introduced by Brabham in 1980 were produced in the USA by Hitco, a division of Armco Steel that had started manufacturing carbon-carbon brakes for military aircraft in the Seventies. Carbon-carbon is difficult and expensive to produce. Essentially it consists of a matrix of carbon/graphite material reinforced with carbon/graphite structural fibres. Production entails putting a woven web of carbonized rayon, pitch or similar fibres in a methane gas filled furnace where, red hot, carbon atoms form on them in a classified process known as carbon vapour deposition. Densification is accomplished by impregnating fibres with carbon during repeated steps at high temperature and the entire process takes many weeks: hence the material's expense. The product has to be machine finished using diamond tooling.

Brabham used 0.7" thick solid carbon-carbon discs supplied direct by Hitco through an 'arm's length' agreement. The discs operated at a significantly higher temperature than conventional cast iron discs – up to 1600 degrees centigrade, not far off the temperature at which carbon-carbon starts to oxidize. It was found impossible to dissipate sufficient heat to maintain an acceptable wear rate on slow circuits so Brabham's discs – ten times as expensive as conventional discs but longer lasting – were somewhat restricted in use. The heat also caused caliper heating problems and Brabham used open bridge Girling four pot calipers which it found well suited. Girling quit racing in 1980 and Brabham bought its remaining stock of calipers.

McLaren had seen the potential of carbon-carbon discs and in '82 started working with French aerospace company SEP which produced its own solid disc. These were first tried by Lauda in a test session at Donington and McLaren International Technical Director John Barnard recalls, 'the performance against iron brakes was stunning. As a measure you are talking about banging on iron brakes at the 100 yard board, with the carbon-carbon brake at the 60 yard board'.

The key to carbon-carbon brake performance being temperature control, McLaren had to constantly rethink ducting and in '83 SEP co-operated in the development of ventilated discs while McLaren designed its own caliper. This featured more surface area, the better to dissipate heat and refinements such as a finned end to the piston to help lower the temperature of the fluid.

By 1984 most Grand Prix teams were toying with carbon-carbon brakes but only Brabham and McLaren had the experience to run them regularly. SEP (which asked to be known thereafter as Carbone Industrie) and Hitco divided the field among themselves, Hitco supplying Brabham direct and other teams via AP Racing. However, Hitco lagged behind in the development of ventilated discs and thus CI had things pretty much its own way through 1985. Nonetheless teams often switched back to cast iron on street circuits and consumption of carbon-carbon discs was higher than anticipated which led to a mid season disc shortage.

By '87 carbon-carbon discs were run everywhere and it was established that the AP Hitco disc was more suited to the new 3.5 litre atmospheric cars since its material was more stable – it had a higher co-efficient of friction cold and increased its co-efficient more gently than the CI disc. The CI disc increased its co-efficient with a bang, but attained a higher value. Hitco discs were thus easier to drive, giving the driver more confidence. They were adequate for turbocar use but experienced drivers preferred the marginally higher performance of the CI disc, given plenty of turbo power to put heat into it.

In 1987 CI introduced an 0.9' rather than 1.0' thick disc, having less mass in an attempt to improve the rate of temperature rise, and steady the cooling rate. Temperatures could become so high that pad and disc wear was unacceptable, though the brake continued working as long as there was still some friction material. Perhaps the worst case of this was Adelaide in '87 where the discs actually wore away. Adelaide in 1985 had witnessed the last Grand Prix win on cast iron brakes.

The advent of carbon-carbon brakes saw cooling much more carefully attended to and the development of special four pot calipers by AP and Brembo. For example, AP had to ditch its lightweight magnesium Formula One caliper (it could not withstand the heat) and develop an aluminium caliper machined from a solid billet rather than cast in two halves. This allowed the use of a grade of aluminium better suited to the heat while doing away with the central joint allowed a thinner caliper that could fit inside a 13" rim leaving more room for insulation between itself and the disc. Special heat insulation inserts were employed while the caliper was wider than was traditionally the case to help keep the sides away from the heat source.

Brembo development followed similar lines and the company even devised a 'shuttle valve' system which helped circulate fluid to avoid heat build up. It was a complex system with separate inward and outward lines for each caliper and the drawback was that there was more to go wrong: failure of one of the valves could mean total brake failure.

An interesting AP development was a twin disc carbon-carbon system, introduced partly to help offset the superior ultimate performance of CI discs. Two floating discs were operated by a single piston on the inside of the caliper so there was no fluid on the outside, helping overcome the heat-to-fluid transfer problem. An altered ratio between master cylinder and piston provided much reduced pedal travel while less pedal effort was found to be another advantage. The performance of the twin disc brake was superior but cooling the outer disc was always a problem. The system thus tended only to be run in qualifying, and the project faded away with the passing of the turbo era.

AP also produced a spin-off cast iron twin disc system which TWR evaluated early in 1986. The team's Sports-Prototype was far heavier than a Formula One car and regularly ran AP cast iron brakes. Again, the twin disc system saw two solid fully floating discs squeezed by a single piston on the inside of the caliper. Less pedal travel and less pedal effort was again evident but knock-off was a problem until the single piston caliper was replaced by twin, balanced calipers. That, of course, added weight and complexity while there was already a problem of cooling with no channel to blow air through. Problems mounted then when Brancatelli was driving one of the inner discs exploded and actually cut through the wheel and monocoque to land inside the tub as the wheel fell off!

TWR abandoned the twin disc project but went on to explore carbon-carbon discs for Sports-Prototype racing. In the mid Eighties the high and narrow working temperature range kept carbon-carbon brakes off Group C and GTP cars but by '87 TWR was having some success with AP/Hitco equipment in testing. The team first raced a carbon-carbon brake on its IMSA GTP car in 1988 and by 1989 carbon-carbon brakes were starting to make inroads into Sports-Prototype racing on both sides of the Atlantic. For example, Mercedes-Sauber ran carbon-carbon discs at almost all '89 races except Le Mans, generally using one set of pads and paired 14" ventilated discs per meeting.

Brands Hatch was one circuit on which carbon-carbon brakes, strangely, did not work well in '89 and the Nissan was one of the few cars not to revert to cast iron brakes for the July World Sports-Prototype Championship meeting. The Nissan RC89 had an excellent Lola chassis and a powerful V8 turbo engine but one major weakness as a package, its braking. The reason for that was a mystery to its race engineers and to its brake suppliers and it helped ensure that Nissan was one of the pioneers of the carbon metallic pad at Le Mans. Thereafter, carbon-carbon brakes gave the RC89 reasonable stopping power and the team could not afford to revert to cast iron brakes, regardless of the problems posed by a specific circuit. It all goes to show that braking performance can be as steeped in black art as underbody aerodynamics. But that is no excuse for not trying to understand the subject. Modern competition car braking systems are based on well proven technology but need to be treated with respect. Brakes can be a matter of life or death, after all.

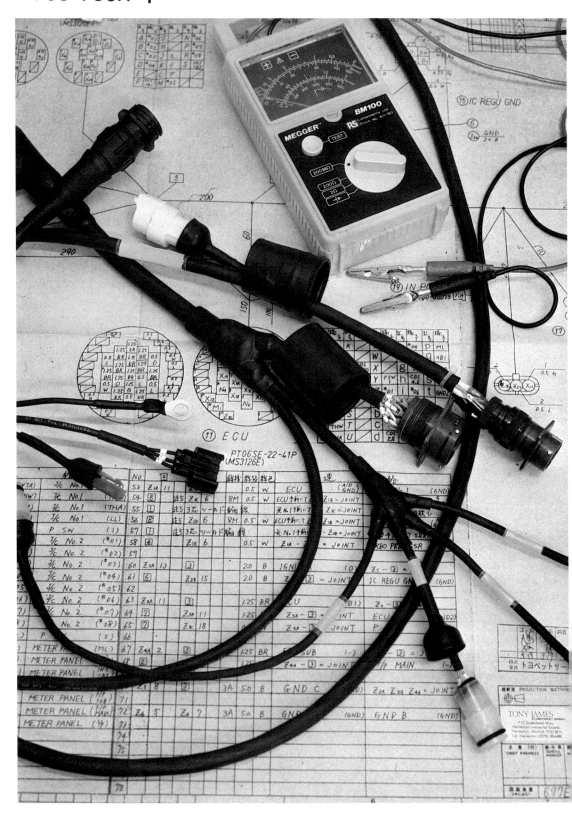

In 1972 Tony James moved to Diss in Norfolk, a town a short distance from the headquarters of Lotus Cars. He had previously served his apprenticeship at his cousin's garage in Leominster, Herefordshire. This garage, in addition to selling motorcycles on a franchise basis, also made specialist machines for road and racing. It was during his time there that the young James discovered an empathy for things electrical. It had also become apparent to him that for every single person in the motor trade proficient in the electrical field there were 50 other mechanics.

An early interest in motorsport had manifested itself while Tony was still at school in the early Sixties, and resulted in him working in his spare time on the cars rallied by British Champion Bill Bengry. Having completed his apprenticeship Tony set out on his own and shortly before the move to East Anglia he was selling BMWs with a local franchise in those last carefree months before the OPEC bubble burst . . .

Soon after arriving in Norfolk, Tony saw a job advertised for an auto-electrician in the service garage of Lotus Cars at Hethel. He got the job. After a year of working on cars for local customers and the national dealer network, a call came for an electrician to go to Team Lotus and sort out an electrical problem. Tony was sent over and after solving the problem on the team transporter he got talking with team members and looked around the workshops.

Sensing a more than average interest from the questions he was asking, Tony was asked if he would be interested in wiring up the Texaco Star Lotus Formula Two cars to be driven by Emerson Fittipaldi and Ronnie Peterson. Tony completed the wiring, working in the evenings and his spare time from his job at Group Lotus. The Texaco Stars proved to be one of Colin Chapman's rare failures and the project was abandoned at the end of 1973.

In the mid-Seventies Tony went back to selling cars, initially at a Ford dealership in Diss. By the end of the decade he was managing the sales department of a large British Leyland outlet, Kitchen Brothers, which was competing locally in rallies. A Mini was campaigned, wiring and preparation courtesy of one Antony James. Phil Denny, an ex-Kitchen Brothers apprentice who had risen to the post of number one mechanic to Mario Andretti, stopped by one day to see the Mini and the conversation soon turned to racing...

At the end of the 1981 season, Tony received a telephone call from Team Lotus Chief Mechanic, Bob Dance, asking if he could work on the wiring of the Formula One cars for the coming year. Lotus had been encountering various headaches with its electrical systems, not least of which was finding great variations in looms from car to car. James decided the best move was to rationalise the situation, particularly as a new type of ignition box was to be used for the new season. A meeting was arranged to discuss his proposals. On seeing what the job entailed, an agreement was reached for Tony to carry out major wiring work on a part-time basis while continuing in the motor trade.

After an intense period of swotting and reacquainting himself with racing car electrical systems, Tony went to the Team Lotus HQ at Ketteringham Hall and built the first loom on the new '82 car. Returning to his home workshop he made a board enabling him to replicate the system independent of the rest of the car, a task that took 15 hours to complete.

Mourning the loss of Colin Chapman in 1983, Team Lotus moved into the turbo era with the Renault V6 engine. The increased complexity of the new engine in comparison to the relative simplicity of the trusty Cosworth DFV used previously made new demands. An intricate wiring harness was necessary to operate systems such as the fuel management which helped to keep the engine operational under the added stresses of turbo-charging.

By mid-season it was obvious that the '83 Lotus 93T was a mobile disaster. In the five-week gap between the Canadian and British Grands Prix, Team Lotus was rejuvenated under the technical direction of the newly-arrived Gerard Ducarouge. The team built a brand-new car to replace the 93T in a matter of weeks. This used the composite monocoque tub of the '82 Cosworth-powered car, a new gearbox and suspension, with the engine and cooling system realigned as per instructions from the Renault factory. The package was clothed in sleek new bodywork.

There was little time for testing before the new 94T model was needed for the British race, which was at Silverstone. One car ran briefly at Hethel and Donington while the second car was untried prior to Silverstone scrutineering. Driving the car with test miles on it, Elio de

Angelis delighted the team and gave the hordes of Lotus fans something to cheer about by recording the fastest time in the first unofficial practice session. By the end of qualifying he was fourth on the grid and hopeful of a good showing in the race. The sister 94T had a rather more difficult time ...

Soon after the start of the first practice session Nigel Mansell's car was afflicted with chronic misfire. In his *Autosport* report Nigel Roebuck described seeing Mansell trundle past ... "I never saw you again after that," I said to Nigel afterwards. "No," he said with a grimace," and what's more, that's as quick as it would go, and that was flat."!

A phone call from Bob Dance alerted Tony to the problems, which a complete chassis strip down and engine change failed to rectify. Between two and four o'clock in the morning the two men went methodically through the car's electrical system on the telephone. Tony suggested possible causes, Bob Dance relayed his comments to the mechanics and the results were passed back to Tony at home in Norfolk.

Eventually the gremlin appeared to have been tracked down and eradicated. Early on the Friday morning Mansell's car disturbed campers by running up and down the Club Straight. All seemed well. A bleary-eyed Bob Dance phoned a bleary-eyed James at 7.30 a.m., to say all systems were 'go'. By the time of the second unofficial qualifying session, Mansell set off from the pits and within minutes the misfire returned. The 94T stuttered back to its garage and Mansell switched to the clumsy 93T that had been brought along as a spare car. At the end of qualifying he was 18th on the grid, four-and-a-half seconds slower than de Angelis.

That evening Lotus personnel were sent to Tony's workshop where they and Tony (who was still working only on a part-time basis for Lotus while running a car sales business during the day) set about building a new wiring loom for Mansell's car. After a second sleepless night, the finished article was ready first thing in the morning. The troubled chassis had been stripped of all its electrical parts and the new loom was fitted by 10.40 a.m.

As the final touches were being made to the car, Tony discovered the cause of the team's two days of woe. The socket on the adaptor plate mounted on the gearbox for the external battery lead to plug into, had been incorrectly wired (this a part not made by Tony). Formula One racing cars depend on their alternator in order to run since the battery used is very small – about the size of a torch battery!

Whenever a car is stationary a large auxiliary battery is plugged into it to stop the car battery going flat, which it would do in a very short time. Because of the incorrect wiring on the adaptor plate socket, each time the powerful and electrically dominant slave battery was plugged in, the polarity on the car was reversed, causing damage to the external diodes which convert the output of the alternator from its raw 'alternating current' to a useable 'direct current' form. When the car was returned to the track it was only a couple of laps before the little car battery, now working without the assistance of the alternator, started to go flat, resulting in misfiring since there was now insufficient power to the fuel management computer.

In his resurrected car Mansell was soon running on the pace. Despite having just the race morning warm-up to familiarise himself with the new chassis, he was 11th quickest. De Angelis meanwhile raised Lotus hopes high by recording fastest warm-up time. In the race the fortunes of qualifying were reversed: de Angelis was out after a single lap with turbo failure while Mansell's car ran like the proverbial train to finish fourth.

As a result of the Silverstone troubles the production of all Team Lotus' electrical peripherals – the irksome adaptor plate included – came under Tony James' wing. Later in 1983, at Tony's instigation, Team Lotus introduced to Formula One racing an aerospace wiring concept – System 25 – with special lightweight wiring capable of withstanding continuous temperatures of 150 degrees Centigrade (and for short periods 350–400 degrees). This wiring is environmentally sealed in heat shrinkable sleeving, leaving no wires visible. Produced by Raychem of Swindon, System 25 wiring has insulation formed by irradiation which changes the molecular structure of the insulating material, making it resistant to high temperatures, as in its altered state it will not melt and drop off the conductor core.

System 25 has subsequently become widely used in Grand Prix and other categories of racing.

At the end of the 1985 season Tony was shown the drawings for the 1986 Lotus 98T and it was obvious that the job of wiring could no longer be done on a part-time basis. Tony James Component Wiring was formed in February 1986, and the business has since grown to the point where it now supplies the electrical requirements of many of the major teams and engine manufacturers in Formula One, CART, Group C and World Championship Rallying.

Some Questions and Answers

Q: What information is required to enable you to manufacture a wiring harness for a client?

A: Sometimes customers will provide detailed drawings to be followed closely but we can also design and produce a harness from scratch. We can also provide systems in bulk. Sometimes we are involved in the installation of the harness but other customers carry out the fitting themselves. We try to be all things to all people. We also like to provide a consultative service for our clients.

Q: How will 1990's harness differ from 1989's?

A: Changes will only result from exhaustive testing with certain teams. Only then will we allow a loom to be used for a full season of racing. Ignition box designs dictate development, obviously weight and size are paramount considerations. Systems are as small and light as possible. In System 25 we are able to use materials that enable us to achieve maximum compactness. Regarding ongoing development, a 1987 loom was recently returned to the factory to be checked over and, by comparison, is worlds apart from the present set up.

Q: What causes electrical fires?

A: Usually a short circuit caused by abrasion of insulation allowing a connection to earth. The resultant overloading causes heat in the conductor, melting the insulation which will catch fire and burn, affecting anything adjacent. The insulation for standard wiring is made by melting PVC pellets and extruding the plastic treacle on to the conductor. This is gradually cooled in a series of water baths of lowering temperatures. When heated this type of insulation will revert to molten state at a relatively low temperature, in fact standard PVC insulation is rated at only 80°C.

In the case of aerospace wiring such as System 25 the insulation has had its molecular structure altered by irradiation which will prevent it remelting and dropping off the conductor. This type of wiring is capable of operating at a continuous temperature of 150°C. The wiring used for the fire extinguisher and life support system is designed to withstand temperatures of 1100°C for a period of five minutes. This is made possible by the use of multi-layer insulation. The outer layers are distanced from the core by laminations of fire resistant materials.

Q: How are the common faults in wiring caused?

A: Usually by a lack of understanding. Chafing and abrasion damage caused by incorrect installation allowing loose wire to rub against bulkheads and such like. This sort of damage does not always result in a fire, it depends on which wire has shorted to earth. A small current wire from a sensor, if affected, may damage the ECU, causing misfire and loss of power.

The arrival in motor racing of so much electronic technology such as engine management, telemetry and active suspension systems, give a wide scope for failures to occur. In the case of the engine management system, which works on pre-set values, it is programmed to react to information gathered from its sensors. If it is given incorrect information due to a fault on the line between sensor and computer, the system malfunctions, adversely affecting the engine.

Some teams' standards of preparation do not seem to have advanced with the technology.

When working my apprenticeship my cousin instilled in me the six Ps – PROPER PREPARATION PREVENTS P*** POOR PERFORMANCE.